Loch Lomond *and* Trossachs

W A L K S

*Compiled by
John Brooks*

JARROLD

Ordnance Survey

Acknowledgements
With thanks to Hamish Brown, Chris and John Harvey, Mr P.M.
Fairweather of Argyll Estates, the officers of Loch Awe, Cowal,
and Aberfoyle Forest Districts, and all others who gave help and
advice. Thanks also to Brenda Stroud who supplied valuable
information used in the preparation of this new edition.

Text:	John Brooks
Photography:	Jarrold Publishing
Editors:	Thomas Albrighton, Donald Greig
Designers:	Brian Skinner, Doug Whitworth
Mapping:	Heather Pearson, Sandy Sims

Series Consultant: Brian Conduit

© Jarrold Publishing and Ordnance Survey 1997
Maps © Crown copyright 1997. The mapping in this guide is
based upon Ordnance Survey ® Pathfinder ®, Outdoor Leisure ™,
Explorer ™ and Travelmaster ® mapping.
Ordnance Survey, Pathfinder and Travelmaster are registered
trade marks and Outdoor Leisure and Explorer are trade marks of
Ordnance Survey, the National Mapping Agency of Great Britain.

Jarrold Publishing   ISBN 0-7117-0572-0

First published 1992
by Jarrold Publishing and Ordnance Survey
Reprinted 1995, 1997
Printed in Great Britain
by Jarrold Book Printing, Thetford. 3/97

Jarrold Publishing,
Whitefriars, Norwich NR3 1TR
Ordnance Survey,
Romsey Road, Southampton SO16 4GU

Front cover:	Culag Farm and Ben Lomond, on the banks of Loch Lomond
Previous page:	Loch Lomond and the Arrochar Alps from Ptarmigan

Contents

Short, easy walks

Walks of modest length, likely to involve some modest uphill walking

More challenging walks which may be longer and/or over more rugged terrain, often with some stiff climbs

Keymap

Walk	Page	Start	Distance	Time	Highest Point
Ardcastle Wood	38	Ardcastle Wood	5 miles (8km)	3 hrs	259ft (79m)
The Ancient Forest below Beinn Dubhchraig	42	Near Tyndrum	6½ miles (10.5km)	4 hrs	1509ft (460m)
Beinn Tharsuinn and Beinn Lochain	61	Lettermay, Lochgoilhead	7 miles (11.3km)	5½ hrs	1624ft (495m)
Ben A'an	34	Near the Trossachs Hotel	2 miles (3.2km)	1½ hrs	1491ft (454m)
The Ben Cruachan Horseshoe	82	Cruachan power station	8 miles (12.9km)	8 hrs	3694ft (1126m)
Ben Ledi	50	Corriechrombie bridge, near Callander	6 miles (9.7km)	3½ hrs	2883ft (879m)
Ben Lomond from Rowardennan	78	Rowardennan	7½ miles (12.1km)	5 hrs	3194ft (974m)
Ben More and Stob Binnein	86	Glen Dochart	10 miles (16.1km)	8 hrs	3851ft (1174m)
Ben Venue	44	Loch Achray hotel	6 miles (9.7km)	4 hrs	2306ft (703m)
Ben Vorlich (Loch Earn)	64	Advorlich, on south side of Loch Earn	7 miles (11.3km)	5½ hrs	3231ft (985m)
The Brack	67	Coilessan, near Ardgartan	9½ miles (15.3km)	5 hrs	2391ft (727m)
Bracklinn Falls and Callendar Craig	36	Callander	4 miles (6.4km)	2 hrs	1125ft (343m)
The Cobbler	71	Head of Loch Long	7 miles (11.3km)	6 hrs	2900ft (884m)
Conic Hill and Balmaha	53	On the West Highland Way	9½ miles (15.3km)	4½ hrs	1148ft (350m)
Creag Bhuidhe	32	Killin	2½ miles (4km)	2 hrs	1673ft (510m)
Cruach Ardrain	75	Glen Falloch, near Crianlarich	7½ miles (12.1km)	6 hrs	3428ft (1046m)
Donich Water and Lochgoilhead	16	Inveronich, Lochgoilhead	2½ miles (4km)	1½ hrs	459ft (140m)
Doune Hill	47	Glenmollochan, at head of Glen Luss	7½ miles (12.1km)	5 hrs	2408ft (734m)
Dùn na Cuaiche, Inverary	30	Inverary Castle	2½ miles (4km)	2 hrs	755ft (230m)
Dunstaffnage Castle	28	Ganavan Bay, near Oban	4 miles (6.4km)	2½ hrs	164ft (50m)
The Fault Trail	26	David Marshall Lodge	3 miles (4.8km)	2½ hrs	1017ft (310m)
Glen Finglas	56	Brig o' Turk	13½ miles (21.5km)	5½ hrs	1968ft (600m)
Inversnaid and Rob Roy's Cave	18	Inversnaid, on east shore of Loch Lomond	2 miles (3.2km)	1½ hrs	492ft (150m)
Isle of Kerrera	40	Kerrara Jetty	6 miles (9.7km)	3½ hrs	328ft (100m)
Killin – Finlarig and Loch Tay	14	Killin	2 miles (3.2km)	1 hr	328ft (100m)
Loch Avich	24	Dalavich, on north-west shore of Loch Awe	5 miles (8km)	2½ hrs	492ft (150m)
Puck's Glen	22	Forestry Commission car park, Puck's Glen	3 miles (4.8km)	2 hrs	721ft (220m)
The Whangie	20	Queen's View, between Drymen and Milngavie	3 miles (4.8km)	1½ hrs	1171ft (357m)

Comments

There is a choice of waymarked routes through the forest here, all of them giving splendid views over Loch Fyne. Keep your eyes peeled as you walk along the shore, as this is a favourite haunt of otters.

Beinn Dubhchraig is a Munro and this route initially takes the path towards the summit. *En route* it passes through remnants of the ancient Caledonian forest, keeping close to a mountain stream.

Beinn Tharsuinn and Beinn Lochain are two rarely climbed summits overlooking Loch Goil. Their ascent calls for some energy and map-reading skill, but in good conditions the scenery is your reward.

Although it is only half the height of a Munro, Ben A'an is a rewarding hill to climb. The views from the top are fabulous, and the unrelenting steepness of the path makes the walk a good test of fitness.

This route should only be attempted by fit, competent walkers as the total height climbed in the traverse exceeds 5000ft (1524m). Some agility is needed to negotiate exposed rock-slabs and gullies.

This is the highest summit of the Trossachs, an imposing mountain which features in many famous views. Although of modest height, Ben Ledi must still be respected – climb it only in good conditions.

The popular route is well-trodden and presents little difficulty. Note that in summer the start of the walk can be reached by ferry from Inverbeg, thus avoiding a long drive up the east shore of the loch.

The ascent of these two mighty peaks demands both stamina and map-reading skill. The view from the top of Ben More takes in half of Scotland and on a clear day you will see England and Ireland too.

The climb to the Ben Venue ridge from the shore of Loch Katrine calls for a fair amount of energy, but the striking views back over the Trossach mountains give an excuse for frequent rests to gain breath.

The summit provides majestic views over Loch Earn to Ben Lawers and beyond. The approach is on a clear path, but the return calls for hillcraft as it descends to a path leading to Glen Vorlich.

There is a choice of routes here and the strenuous will probably prefer to visit The Brack (2582ft/787m). The longer circuit only calls for two steepish climbs and the views are hardly less striking.

There are few taxing gradients on this walk which takes in fine views and a famous waterfall. Try to walk this route after heavy rain, when the Keltie Water thunders through a series of cataracts.

The Cobbler –the summit of Ben Arthur – has a contorted shape which has made it the best-known Trossachs mountain. Its popularity has led to path erosion and the going is quite difficult near the top.

The West Highland Way is followed through forest and moorland to Conic Hill, which rivals Ben Lomond as a viewpoint. The return from Balmaha initially follows the main road which has a wide footpath.

This hill, rising to the west of Killin, gives an outstanding view of Loch Tay and its surrounding peaks. From the summit the route uses an old peat road (overgrown and moist in places) for the return.

Soon after the start there is a gruelling climb up Grey Height, at the far end of the ridge to Cruach Ardrain. This ridge-walk to the Munro is exciting, as is the return route beside a refreshing burn.

The climax of this short and undemanding walk is a series of waterfalls situated in a beautiful sylvan glen. It is a wonderful place to picnic on a hot day.

The Luss Hills are farmed for sheep so dogs are unwelcome. Doune Hill gives views to all points of the compass, and the walk along the ridge from Beinn Eich is immensely enjoyable.

The short climb up to this knoll gives grand views over Loch Fyne. However in bygone days it was the view into the mouths of the three nearby glens that made it important to the Campbell lookouts.

At one point on the outward path, agility is called for in crossing a gully, but otherwise the going is easy, with superb views. The castle was a Campbell stronghold, occupied by them until a fire in 1810.

This forest trail follows part of the Highland Boundary Fault; a leaflet available from David Marshall Lodge explains local geology. The viewpoint shows all the major summits of the Southern Highlands.

This is a lengthy walk on clear tracks taking you into the heart of very wild country. Note that the tracks were made for stalking deer: in the season check that shooting is not taking place on the hill.

The West Highland Way is followed along a remote Loch Lomond shore to the famous cave supposed to have been a hideout of Rob Roy. The return climbs a path to a grand viewpoint.

Kerrera has a special romantic atmosphere and this makes the effort of getting there worthwhile. Its scenery is wild and beautiful, with the ruined Gylen Castle adding to the romance.

A disused railway track leads to a path through lochside and riverside meadows which may become waterlogged after heavy rain. This makes a delightful evening stroll.

The switchback nature of this forest walk is not apparent from the map, and may surprise the unwary. However the energy expended proves worthwhile when you reach the lonely shore of Loch Avich.

The glen contains a picturesque series of waterfalls and thus the walk will be most enjoyable after rainfall. Note that the path in the upper glen is steep, narrow, and often slippery.

The Whangie is an impressive canyon of tumbled rocks which has long puzzled geologists. After threading through it, the path climbs Auchineden Hill, overlooking the Clyde Valley and Loch Lomond.

Introduction to the Loch Lomond and Trossachs area

Walking in Scotland is quite different from walking south of the border, and though the Southern Highlands may sound tame at first compared with the mountainous regions further to the north, within them are peaks which deserve every respect. In England there are only eight summits which top 3000ft (914m) while in Scotland there are 277, with 45 of those lying within the Southern Highlands. Although this book does not embrace the mountains to the north of Glen Dochart and Loch Tay (where Ben Lawers, the monarch of the Southern Highlands, is situated), there are challenges enough in the area covered. The two most demanding walks described in this Pathfinder Guide feature ridge walks involving a total ascent well in excess of 5000ft (1500m) in each instance.

Walkers in Scotland will inevitably become acquainted with the term 'Munro', which simply indicates one of the 277 distinct Scottish mountains whose summits top 3000ft (914m). The name is taken from that of the 19th-century Scottish climber who first listed them, and now it is a popular pursuit for many to try to 'bag' them all, perhaps several times over. Less known, and perhaps more fun, are the 'Corbetts', the summits of which lie between 2500ft and the magic 3000ft (762m and 914m). They lie in equally remote parts of Scotland and, because they are usually relatively unfrequented, present a challenge as formidable as many Munros. Altogether there are 223 Corbetts.

Even on the lesser walks visitors from south of the border will notice important differences from walking at home. Most notably there is little waymarking to be seen away from the routes adopted by the Forestry Commission and a few large estates such as Inveraray. Several of these forest and estate walks are featured in the early pages of this book. However, some of the moderately demanding routes (colour-coded blue) and most of the really challenging ones (colour-coded orange) involve sections over open hillside where there are few indications of paths other than those made by sheep.

A secluded waterfall on the Fault Trail

In Scotland it is very difficult to devise the sort of circular footpath routes which are popular with southern walkers. The shepherd's daily walk nearly always covers different ground and he usually heads straight up or down the hillside, either on foot or using an all-terrain vehicle. It is the sheep rather than the shepherd who make the paths and their aims are usually not in sympathy with those of the hill-walker. The ancient drovers' routes are more useful and abound in the Highlands; the herds were driven through mountain passes (*bealach* is the Gaelic word for these, and will frequently be seen on maps) either to market or to fresh pastures. New roads built for the Land Rovers of modern-day stalkers often follow these traditional routes.

The Southern Highlands have always been the playground of outdoor enthusiasts from Glasgow and the other industrial and mining towns of the Clyde and Forth valleys. The building of railways brought the mountains within reach of workers who on Sundays took the trains to places like Arrochar or Crianlarich and spent the day on the hills. Walking and climbing became the recreational pursuits of many thousands of ordinary people who lived in the tenements and back-to-backs. Instead of the circular routes popular today, the walking then was most often across country from station to station and often incorporated a couple of Munros. Certainly the contrast between the flat, smoky expanse of the industrial plain and the mountainous wilderness just to the north could hardly have been greater, and the latter could be reached from many nearby urban areas within an hour.

Of course this contrast is due to geology. The line between highlands and lowlands follows that of an enormous earth movement which took place some 400 million years ago; faint echoes of this cataclysmic event are still felt here occasionally as very mild earthquakes. To the south of the fault the rock is younger and softer, being mainly sedimentary sandstones of the Devonian and Carboniferous eras. In places volcanic activity burst through these sediments and altered them, creating highland outliers such as the Campsie and Ochil hills.

The easiest way to gain an understanding of the geology of the area is to follow Walk 7 (The Fault Trail), where the Forestry Commission have taken pains to give storyboard explanations about the Highland Boundary Fault on the ground where the events happened. This is both an enjoyable and very educational route.

Long after the formation of this fault, during the final stages of the last Ice Age (about 10,000 years ago), glaciation wrought the final geological changes. Feeder glaciers from the mountains to the north of the Forth and Clyde brought rock and gravel debris, which was added to the spoil of the enormous glacier that occupied this central rift. These glaciers smoothed and steepened the corries of the mountains in their upper parts, and chiselled out broader valleys as they descended. Later, as they melted, they

Introduction

dumped their debris, leaving heaps of highland rock in locations far away from where it originated. Sometimes, where there was an upstanding volcanic extrusion, the glacier left a 'crag and tail', the tail being the moraine, the material torn from mountainsides far distant and piled up behind the crag like the tail of a comet, a gentle slope descending from the top of the steep rock face that had faced the glacier.

Thus there can be no disputing that the area covered by this book lies within the Highlands. At its heart is the small area known as the Trossachs – by rights just the richly wooded glen between Lochs Katrine and Achray, but usually taken to describe a tract of country extending northwards from Aberfoyle to include Lochs Ard, Katrine, Achray and Venachar. It is the district's tree-fringed lochs, rather than the hills which surround them, which give it its rare beauty and character. The name 'Trossachs' is derived from the Gaelic and means 'bristly country'. The scenery here is particularly spectacular when clothed in the colours of autumn.

Loch Lomond lies to the west of the Trossachs and shares with them the aura of romance that was bestowed on the district firstly by Wordsworth and Coleridge but then more famously by Sir Walter Scott, who made the Trossachs the setting for *The Lady of the Lake* and *Rob Roy*. Both areas suffer from being overwhelmed by tourists in the holiday season but comparatively few venture far from the lochside roads, and peace and beauty can readily be found in the hills, especially away from the more famous heights.

Further to the west again Loch Fyne stretches its fingers towards the heart of the Highlands. Here again there are many delightful spots to explore where you will be unlikely to encounter even another walker. Only one walk (to the west of Inveraray) is suggested by Loch Fyne, but there could be a bookful. The same goes for the countryside to the north and west. Ben Cruachan dominates here, even from the coast, and presents one of the best ridges for walking anywhere in the Highlands. Two seaside walks are also included, to give variety and, perhaps, a welcome alternative if the weather is bad over the tops.

The eastern extremity of the area covered here is dominated by Loch Earn's Ben Vorlich in much the same way that Ben Cruachan rules to the west. To the south-east an exploration of the strange geological feature known as The Whangie gives yet another perspective of the mountains of the Southern Highlands, as well as a view over the vast plains of the Clyde and Forth.

Although much of the countryside lies at a lower level and is less forbidding than, say, that surrounding Glen Coe, nevertheless considerable heights lie within it, and none of the Munros of the Southern Highlands should be thought of as easy. Popular hills like Ben Lomond or The Cobbler are busy with walkers throughout the summer, and though these demand respect, the less frequented mountains are more dangerous simply because

Loch Etive and Appin from Ben Cruachan

if accidents do happen here it is unlikely that there will be anyone nearby to give assistance or go for help. In these Pathfinder guides the walks are graded in difficulty, beginning with the easy ones and ending with the most demanding in terms of both stamina and navigation. Make no mistake: the latter routes given here are not for the casual walker in trainers and T-shirt. They are immensely enjoyable and satisfying, but should only be undertaken in good conditions, by fit walkers who are well equipped. The times given at the start of each walk are only approximations, and adequate time must be allowed to take account of slight accidents of navigation or changes in the weather. It is no joke to be benighted and lost on the higher slopes of Ben More or Cruachan even in good conditions, and each year people lose their lives on comparatively easy hills which seem to offer few hazards.

These disasters, which often stem from seemingly trivial mishaps, are made far less likely if you take sensible equipment. Boots are essential, even though you may be able to escape with dry feet on one or two of the easier walks in a dry summer; good, comfortable boots not only keep your feet dry but also support the ankles, which can easily be turned on slippery rocks. A windproof, waterproof jacket should also be carried. Though the day may seem blisteringly hot when you set out, by the time you reach the 3000-ft (914m) contour the temperature may well have dropped by more than ten degrees, and the wind will bring an unwelcome chill rather than the comforting coolness looked for when you were energetically climbing.

Introduction

On the other hand, many casualties on the tops of mountains are the result of heat exhaustion and dehydration, so be sure to have a water-bottle with you and drink water rather than soft drinks, which will increase your thirst rather than assuage it. A beer hidden in a burn near the start of the walk is something to look forward to on the way down.

The food you carry up mountains should be light, refreshing and nourishing: do not take salty items like potato crisps which anyway, by the time you get to the top, will be pulverised into unpalatable crumbs. Sweet things also increase thirst; apples, nuts and raisins are ideal.

Take relevant maps to complement this guide (see page 95). The appropriate 1:50 000 sheet will allow you to work out where you are in relation to more distant landmarks, and a compass (essential for the more difficult walks) not only tells where you are heading but enables you to pinpoint your own position and identify mountains on the horizon. Learn how to use the compass by practising when you are out on the easier routes. A whistle and first-aid kit complete emergency gear (see the section entitled *Safety on the hills* on page 93).

Many walkers accustomed to the Highlands would add an anti-insect cream or ointment to this list. The midge (*Culicoides impunctatus*) is a curse which is seldom mentioned by tourist literature. It may be tiny but it is a man-eater and it particularly likes damp, misty conditions. It is unlikely to be encountered in strong sunshine or on windy days. The common fly is another plague, but unlike the midge this seems to prefer sunshine. It is particularly annoying to photographers, who find it difficult to work with flies swarming around the camera lens. A figure prancing on a mountain-top will invariably be a photographer attempting to distract the beasts.

Although it is difficult to miss the 'tourist routes' up popular hills such as (again) The Cobbler or Ben Lomond, be warned that the popular way of high-level walking in Scotland, up to and on top of the ridges, often entails choosing your own way over rough and virtually pathless ground. The right to take one's own route at will over the open land of the hill has been important to generations of walkers and climbers in Scotland. It is an unwritten right, however, and depends on goodwill between walkers and landowners. Thus walkers must pay regard to sporting or agricultural interests. Only in a few instances will these clash with free access. In lambing time walkers with dogs will not be welcome, however closely controlled the dogs may be. In the shooting season hills will be closed when stalking is taking place (the telephone numbers of stalkers are included in the introductions to routes where difficulties are most likely to occur).

Deer-stalking is an emotive topic and its main reason is often overlooked. Deer are basically forest animals and with the destruction of their original habitat in the unregimented forests they are now having to live in very hard, unnatural conditions. They often have to be fed and their numbers controlled by culling, otherwise they starve to death. Nobody has devised a better control system than simply shooting the weaker, poorer animals, which is in fact what happens.

Unfortunately many estates under-cull, and in a wet late springtime you may well come upon the sad spectacle of dead deer. The culling of the stags, from mid-August to the end of the third week in October, is a vital part of an estate's economy, and keeps the local herd going. For this reason (and, of course, to avoid danger to themselves) at this time walkers should keep away from areas being stalked.

Looking across Loch Katrine to Ben A'an

The hinds (females) are culled by the keepers over the winter when there are fewer people on the hills, but the same courtesy is expected. For instance, if a Land Rover is seen at a corrie mouth it is likely that shooting is taking place, and it would be very selfish of the walker to barge in and ruin a day's work. Calving time is June and a dappled calf found on a hillside should *not* be touched. It is not abandoned and the returning hind may reject her calf if it smells of humans.

This book covers a vast area of countryside within which, of course, changes are taking place all the time. New landowners may put up deer fences, which force detours, or plant forests, which can prevent access to the tops altogether. Hopefully such restrictions will not be encountered on any of the routes suggested here.

However, do not be put off by these strictures, and above all remember that it is not obligatory to walk any route in its entirety. The approaches to many of the mountains are frequently the best parts of the walk, with the final struggle to the summit often satisfying pride more than anything else. Should you choose to descend the way you have climbed up you will have the view in front of you: the further up you go, the longer this will last.

Killin – Finlarig and Loch Tay

Start	Killin
Distance	2 miles (3.2km)
Approximate time	1 hour
Parking	Municipal car park at north end of village
Refreshments	Pubs and tearooms in Killin
Ordnance Survey maps	Landranger 51 (Loch Tay) and Pathfinder 334, NN 43/53 (Killin)

There can be no doubt that this is the most level walk featured in these pages. It follows the line of the old railway which once ran from the village to a pier at the head of Loch Tay where passengers would disembark on to a steamer. When the loch is reached a return is made by loch- and riverside meadows to Killin, which means 'long village' – it extends for more than a mile (1.6km) north to south. This makes a relaxing evening stroll after energetic walking elsewhere, though the meadows may be wet after prolonged rain.

The old railway which once linked Killin with a steamer pier is now a public walkway and can be joined at the car park. Turn north (left) on to its trackbed and cross the iron bridge over the River Lochay. Meall Garbh is the splendid mountain dominating the landscape ahead.

Trees effectively hide the ruins of Finlarig Castle, on a hillock on the left, which was the headquarters of the Campbells in Breadalbane after they bought the Auchmore lands in the fifteenth century. A gruesome feature of the ruins is the 'beheading pit' where the Campbells disposed of prisoners they were unable to ransom. Before the Campbells came to the district this was MacNab land, and they continued to live here, somewhat uneasily, after they had finally mortgaged most of their estate to the 6th laird in 1553. The MacNabs lived in a fine house close to the castle and their relationship with their powerful neighbours was ever stormy. General Monk had to intervene to prevent violence between them during the Commonwealth.

Beyond Finlarig the track runs on an embankment parallel to a road on its left. On the right there are disused telegraph poles in the undergrowth and occasionally there are old sleepers underfoot too. Gradually the shore of the loch draws nearer; turn off the railway through a kissing-gate on the right Ⓐ to reach a lovely path which follows the edge of the loch. The shoreline is fringed by sandy beaches backed by grand trees, many of them oaks. There is a richly wooded island where the two rivers flow into Loch Tay,

The Falls of Dochart are at the entrance to Killin village

and here the path turns westwards to return to the bridge crossed earlier.

Recross the bridge and then, if time permits, turn left off the old railway **B** to follow another riverbank path to reach the mouth of the River Dochart. The water-meadows support a grand variety of wildlife – dippers and waders will be seen in the river, while hares enjoy grazing the rich grassland.

The path soon reaches the railway again, this time by an imposing masonry bridge **C** (note that the five arches are concrete, one of the first examples in Britain of this material's use in such work). Turn back from the bridge along the old railway to reach the car park, deviating briefly from the track to pass through the site of the station, later used as a cattle market. ●

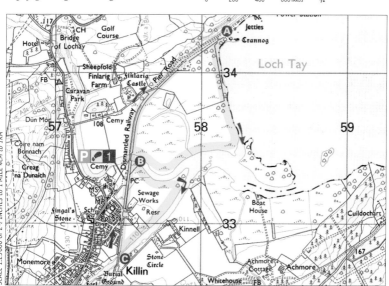

Donich Water and Lochgoilhead

Start	Inveronich, Lochgoilhead
Distance	2½ miles (4km)
Approximate time	1½ hours
Parking	Follow forestry walk symbol as you enter Lochgoilhead from north on B839, and park in forestry car park at Inveronich Farm
Refreshments	Pub and restaurants at Lochgoilhead
Ordnance Survey maps	Landranger 56 (Loch Lomond & Inveraray) and Pathfinder 368, NN 20/30 (Arrochar & Ben Lomond)

A very pleasant short walk which leads to a sylvan gem – a rock pool the size of a swimming pool, fed by waterfalls. More falls are close by, and there can be few more delightful places to picnic. Alternatively refreshment can be obtained by detouring into Lochgoilhead on the way back. Note that this route can be used to extend Walk 23 to the village.

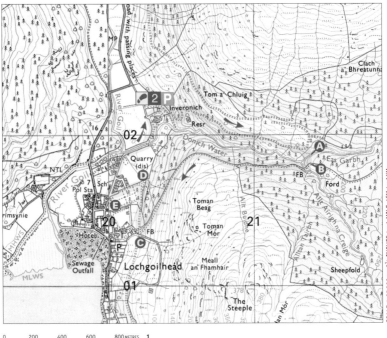

Take the steep path from the farm into the forest (waymarked 'DW', meaning Donich Water). This is a quiet hillside track through mixed forest with occasional views to the right over the loch. The sound of the rushing stream drifts up from below as the path levels out after the initial steep climb. The hill to the right is The Steeple (why does it bear a Sassenach name?).

Within half an hour the path twists down to the stream below, crossing the first of two bridges above a waterfall and pool **Ⓐ**. This bridge spans Eas Garbh, the following one Allt Airigh na Creige: the two streams join together at this point to make Donich Water. The right of way from Glen Croe is joined just before the second footbridge. Turn right on to this **Ⓑ** to cross over the bridge and view another lovely rock pool which has three cataracts spilling into it.

Lochgoilhead

The walk back is hardly less pleasing: it passes through shady woodland at first with the stream close by, and then emerges on to the open hill with the forest to the right. (There is a concealed footpath on the right which cuts off a hairpin bend above Lochgoilhead, but since at the time of writing it is marked only by a tin can on a post it seems risky to recommend it. The going on the longer route is pleasant anyway.)

Turn sharply to the right when the track meets another just before the village **Ⓒ** (or descend to Lochgoilhead if you seek refreshments). Turn left when the way ahead ends at a gate **Ⓓ** and walk past Lochgoilhead car park (another possible starting point for this route), turning right at the end of the road **Ⓔ** to pass the school and a group of houses. After the doctor's surgery the road becomes a path bearing right and leading to an electricity sub-station and then to a bridge over Donich Water. Cross this to return to Inveronich. ●

Inversnaid and Rob Roy's Cave

Start	Inversnaid, on east shore of Loch Lomond
Distance	2 miles (3.2km)
Approximate time	1½ hours
Parking	Car park at Inversnaid pier
Refreshments	Inversnaid Hotel
Ordnance Survey maps	Landranger 56 (Loch Lomond & Inveraray) and Outdoor Leisure 39 (Loch Lomond)

Rob Roy had many caves in the area covered by this book, but this is one of the best known, as it is pointed out to passengers aboard Loch Lomond pleasure steamers. This walk can be enjoyed by those using the ferry from Tarbet to Inversnaid, though the drive up the long road to Inversnaid, past Loch Chon and Loch Ard, is memorably beautiful. The route includes an enticing section of the West Highland Way, and a detour on the way back through RSPB woodland gives superb views of Loch Lomond and the surrounding hills.

Illustrated leaflets on the RSPB reserve are available at the start of the walk or from the hotel. Look at the waterfall at the south end of the car park before setting out. It is supposed to have inspired Wordsworth's lines 'To a Highland Girl'. Later, Gerard Manley Hopkins also immortalised Inversnaid in verse:

What would the world be once bereft
Of wet and wilderness...

Some backpackers on the West Highland Way, passing by on a particularly moist day, might regard his sentiments with some cynicism.

Follow the West Highland Way northwards from the car park. Birch and oak trees frame views of the loch from the first, though the power station and traffic noise on the ever-busy main road are intrusive. The broad, well-surfaced path narrows and is rougher underfoot after the boathouse is reached Ⓐ and two burns are crossed. Look for members of the famous Loch Lomond herd of wild goats here. In fact they are not at all shy and kept King Robert the Bruce warm when, a fugitive, he sheltered in a cave here. In better times, remembering their companionship, he passed a law allowing free grazing for these goats.

In places steep crags crowd above the path, which soon comes to a great tumble of rocks below even higher crags. Steps have been made to help walkers climb this obstacle, but care is still needed, especially if the stone is wet. More steps lead down on the far side of the massive pile of rocks, and here a sign points out a path to the left

SCALE 1:25 000 or 2½ INCHES to 1 MILE 4CM to 1KM

```
0    200   400   600   800 METRES  1
                                    KILOMETRES
                                    MILES
0    200   400   600 YARDS    ½
```

are for the benefit of boat passengers. The cave itself is a disappointment anyway, being just a larger cleft amongst the tumbled rocks. However, the spot is ruggedly beautiful and deserves its legacy of romance.

Unless you would like to explore further along the West Highland Way (though be warned that the going gets wetter further north) turn back along the way you have come. When you hear the rushing waters of a burn, but before reaching it, look for steps ascending on the left **C**. Take this detour (which entails quite a long climb) to explore an RSPB reserve embracing an area of woodland covering the hillside above the loch. You will see many nesting-boxes in the trees; at the right time of year these may house pied flycatchers, which are becoming rare in these parts. Other birds to be seen in spring and summer include great spotted woodpeckers, various warblers and pipits, and birds of prey such as kestrels and buzzards. There are seats in two strategic positions which give wonderful views over the loch and make the strenuous climb worth while.

The path descends through the woods to reach the West Highland Way again close to the boathouse **A**. Turn left to pass the boathouse and return to the starting point at Inversnaid. ●

leading to Rob Roy's Cave **B**, which may well have been the one used earlier by King Robert.

Only the sure-footed should attempt the scramble above the water to reach the cave. The enormous white letters painted on the rock above its entrance

Loch Lomond from the RSPB path

The Whangie

Start	Queen's View, on A809 between Drymen and Milngavie
Distance	3 miles (4.8km)
Approximate time	1½ hours
Parking	Queen's View car park
Refreshments	None
Ordnance Survey maps	Landranger 64 (Glasgow) and Outdoor Leisure 39 (Loch Lomond)

Opinion is divided on the nature of the geological process which caused the Whangie, a remarkable canyon reached by a short but scenically spectacular walk. Beyond the Whangie the path climbs up to a splendid viewpoint on Auchineden Hill which overlooks the Clyde Valley in one direction and Loch Lomond in the other.

A plaque at the start puts forward two geological explanations for the formation of the Whangie (either glacial plucking or earthquake), plus the more attractive myth that it was caused by the Devil flicking his tail in anticipation of pleasures in store as he flew over Stockie Muir on his way to attend a Witches' Sabbath.

At the start there is a staircase of old wooden railway sleepers, designed to

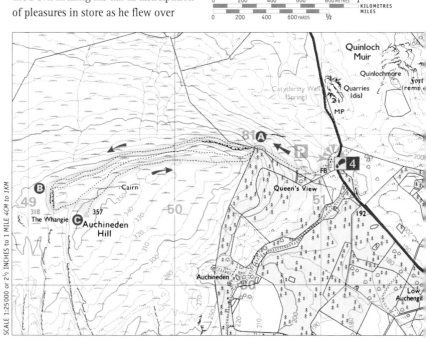

protect the hillside from excessive erosion (the land is under the care of the National Trust for Scotland). After this, continue climbing the hill to a stile Ⓐ at the top corner of the wood. Cross the stile and take the lower path keeping close to the fence. The dramatic impact of the Whangie is best experienced if, when alternatives are offered; you keep to the lower path on every occasion. This path is vague when it threads through a small boulder-field below a cliff-face. Keep to the lower edge of the boulders, away from the base of the cliff. Loch Lomond can be seen in the distance. The fence swings away from here, but remains in sight.

The next rocky outcrop on the skyline is the Wee Whangie which is a sort of trailer for the real thing. None the less it provides a good scramble and squeeze for children.

The Whangie

It is followed by another boulder-field overlooked by rock pinnacles. Continue on the lowest path around the shoulder of the hill without gaining much height. Suddenly the steeples and pinnacles of the Whangie itself appear, and the path winds beneath the faces beloved by rock-climbers Ⓑ. Even though the heights are very modest, there are several routes which demand of the climber considerable skill and agility.

On the far side of the fissure the path climbs round the hill (note the reservoir on the right) and passes into a more conventional gorge; at the top of this bear right on a distinct path which leads up to the triangulation pillar on top of Auchineden Hill Ⓒ. On a clear day it is an excellent place for hill-spotting: Ben Lomond can hardly be missed but many other summits will not be quite as easy to identify.

From the triangulation pillar, turn north-east to walk along a well-used path passing well to the left of the cairn. There are wide views ahead as the path drops down the hillside, soon returning to the stile Ⓐ which gave access to the hill near the start. ●

Puck's Glen

Start	Forestry Commission car park, Puck's Glen
Distance	3 miles (4.8km)
Approximate time	2 hours
Parking	Forestry Commission car park on east side of A815 Strachur – Dunoon road, a mile (1.6km) south of the Younger Botanic Garden, Benmore
Refreshments	Pubs at Kilmun and Sandbank
Ordnance Survey maps	Landranger 56 (Loch Lomond & Inveraray) and Pathfinder 389, NS 08/18 (Sandbank & Holy Loch)

This short walk can easily be extended to include the Black Gates Walk, which almost adjoins it to the north, or the walks through the arboretum at Kilmun. A visit to the Younger Botanic Garden, just a mile (1.6km) to the north, is recommended for those with an interest in plants and fine trees. Puck's Glen itself contains a large number of specimen trees and was once part of the demesne of the Younger residence, Benmore. However, the prime attraction of the walk is the romantic glen with its ravines and series of cascades, which some may feel more likely to be haunted by trolls than fairies.

Puck's Glen

Take the path (waymarked by posts with red tops) directly uphill from the car park, climbing steeply through the forest to reach the side of Puck's Glen above two footbridges **A**. There is a choice of paths here: you may bear right up some stone steps which once led to a folly on top of the hill (it has been reconstructed in the garden at Benmore), or you may descend to the bottom of the glen and walk up beside the tumbling burn (though this will mean walking this part of the route again later on).

Taking the detour from the glen up the steps is interesting when you reflect that ladies visiting Benmore in Victorian times would have been expected to climb up here in wide crinolines.

Bear right on reaching the bottom of the glen after descending the stone steps from the site of the folly. Take care on the last section below a sheer rock-face where the steps are especially steep and slippery. The path by the side of the Eas Mór climbs steadily to reach a forest track **B**: should you wish to extend the walk to Kilmun you will turn right here to follow this track southwards. You will also see a sign pointing to the right to a viewpoint. Although this gives good views of Glen Massan and its hills, photographers will be disappointed to see the concrete-covered reservoir in the foreground.

To continue the main walk, go straight over the forest track and follow the path by the burn to the upper glen. It is narrow and more difficult than that lower down. Fallen trees are frequent obstacles and the going is often steep, narrow and slippery. For all this the rare beauty of the ravine is unique, and greatly enhanced if the burn is in flood. Near the top a rope on the left gives a welcome handhold, for the drop on the other side is precipitous.

The unwaymarked hill-route to Gairletter and Loch Long continues to follow the Eas Mór at the top of the forest **C**. However, the present walk takes the path to the left, towards Black

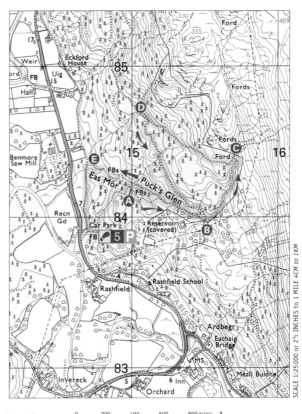

SCALE 1:25000 or 2½ INCHES to 1 MILE 4CM to 1KM

Gates, which is narrow and wet at times; it descends gently down the hill with mature trees to the left and new planting to the right allowing views of the open hill.

Turn to the left when this path meets with a forest track **D**. About 10 or 15 minutes' walking brings you back to **B**, where you turn right to follow the path all the way down to the bridges at the very foot of the glen. Note the stainless-steel plaque mounted on a bare rock-face, which acknowledges the vital role played by the Manpower Services Commission in creating this path. With its innumerable footbridges over the glen this is indeed a remarkable achievement.

Turn to the left when the path ends at a redundant part of the main road **E**, and follow this back to the car park. ●

Loch Avich

Start	Dalavich, on the north-west shore of Loch Awe
Distance	5 miles (8km)
Approximate time	2½ hours
Parking	Forestry Commission picnic site at Barnaline, Dalavich
Refreshments	Tearoom at Inverinan, 3 miles (4.8km) north-east of Dalavich
Ordnance Survey maps	Landranger 55 (Lochgilphead) and Pathfinder 355, NM 81/91 (Kilmelford)

The Forestry Commission have gone to great trouble and expense to attract the public to their walks from Dalavich and Inverinan. Each of these walks has its own appeal: the Loch Avich route featured here is one of the most strenuous, following a tortuous switchback route to the unfrequented south shore of the loch before returning via the path following the River Avich. It is easy to extend the walk to visit the famous waterfall, waymarked as the Avich Falls Walk. Although the path has been greatly improved recently, it can still be muddy in places.

From the car park follow the forestry road uphill; the waterfall can be heard below. Bear left at the junction **A** following the yellow waymark. To the left is the Dalavich Oakwood, where a nature reserve has been established to preserve part of the broadleaved woodland which once covered much of the Loch Awe hillside; this is an important habitat for animals, birds and insects. The oakwood provided charcoal for the Bonawe iron-smelting furnace, and in the early 19th century 600 men were employed in the forests producing the 1000 tons (1016 tonnes) needed each year. Some of the small quantity of oak now harvested from the woods is used for smoking fish.

Further on a thinning of conifers allows a view of Loch Awe; an even better one is obtained from a knoll

SCALE 1:25000 or 2½ INCHES to 1 MILE 4CM to 1KM

reached via a waymarked diversion. The forest road continues on a level course for another $\frac{1}{2}$ mile (800m) until, about $1\frac{1}{2}$ miles (2.4km) after the start, it bears to the left and descends. Follow the footprint symbol to the right here **B** on to a lesser, embanked track which follows the uneven ground like a big dipper and makes exhilarating walking.

The path soon comes to a remarkable natural amphitheatre known as the Dry Loch **C**. Plans are advanced to flood this drained lochan again and create a richer wildlife habitat and scenic asset. Beyond this there are some crumbling stone walls which once belonged to the fields and houses of old crofts. Trees flourish on this land, which was under cultivation two centuries ago. From here to Loch Avich a wide variety of coniferous species have been planted and some stray broadleaved trees have also become established. Look out for the rare and distinctive Japanese cedar (*Cryptomeria*), an experimental planting of the 1950s.

The path descends steeply to reach the shore of Loch Avich by a picturesque red-roofed fishing hut **D**. It takes about an hour to reach this point,

The Dry Loch

the start of a delightful section of the route close to the shore of the loch. The trees here are oak, ash and birch, which provide a colourful foreground in spring and autumn. There is an imposing hunting lodge on the other side of the loch (Lochavich House). The path continues to pursue its switchback style and it seems no time before the bank of the River Avich is reached **E**.

The path now follows the river downstream through woodland which is quite dense at times. The waterfall is heard but never seen (though easily visited by using another forestry trail). When the original forest road is reached turn left to return to the car park. ●

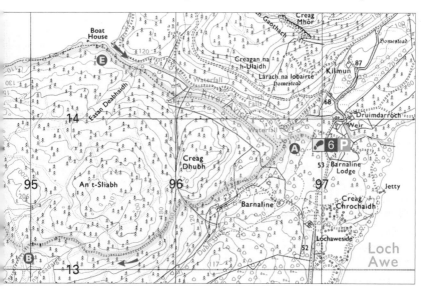

The Fault Trail

Start	David Marshall Lodge, Aberfoyle (Visitor Centre for the Queen Elizabeth Forest Park)
Distance	3 miles (4.8km)
Approximate time	2½ hours
Parking	Forestry Commission car park at David Marshall Lodge off A821 ½ mile (800m) north of Aberfoyle
Refreshments	Tearoom at David Marshall Lodge
Ordnance Survey maps	Landranger 57 (Stirling & The Trossachs) and Explorer 11 (The Trossachs)

Anyone wishing to understand the geology of the area should walk this route in Achray Forest which covers an important part of the Highland Boundary Fault (a major geological event which took place 390 million years ago). Apart from several excellent scenic features (waterfalls and a superb viewpoint being the most outstanding) it is the explanatory storyboards placed at various points of interest which give the walk its fascination. An excellent leaflet on the Fault Trail is available from the Lodge.

Take the path on the left side of the Lodge, initially following the Waterfall Trail. However, this soon goes its separate way, and the Highland

David Marshall Lodge

Boundary Fault Trail (which has distinctive blue waymarks) leads over a raised timber walkway before dropping down to the stream with its 55-ft (16.5m) waterfall **A**. Cross the bridge below the waterfall and then turn left

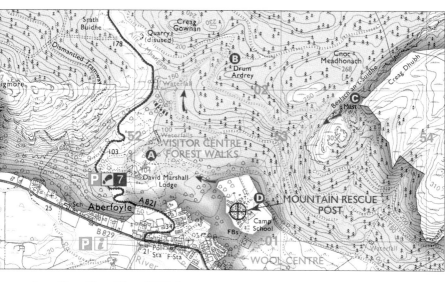

SCALE 1:25 000 or 2½ INCHES to 1 MILE 4CM to 1KM

0	200	400	600	800 METRES	1	
						KILOMETRES
						MILES
0	200	400	600 YARDS	½		

up a forest track (keep a sharp lookout for fast-moving mountain-bikers here). The information posts on this section explain about slate and tree-planting.

Bear left at the track junction and climb until, with the sound of a waterfall close by, you see a blue waymark pointing down into the woods on the left. This allows a pleasant diversion from the forest track, leading down to the side of a burn. Turn right to follow this upstream to another information board, this one telling of the 'enduring dynamics of geology'. To illustrate the point there is a beautifully secluded little waterfall close by. Return to the main track and turn left to continue climbing.

At a major track junction **B** (the theme here is the ever-active earth) turn sharply to the right to pass an exposure of Leny Grit, a typical rock of the Southern Highlands, being metamorphosed sand and gravel. After this the track bends to the left and drops, before resuming its ascent; it is a considerable distance to the next information board (Volcanic Hills), where there is a seat and a fine view south to the Campsie Hills. The Highland Boundary Fault is to be found a little further on, between two boards placed close together. A nice touch here is the shape of the post bearing the information board about the Fault, the reversed Z representing the movement of the two parts of the earth's crust.

The radio mast can now be clearly seen ahead above Lime Craig Quarry, where limestone was worked until about 130 years ago. Move on to the next information board and having read its content turn left at the bottom of the quarry to climb to the hill **C** above, a wonderful viewpoint for all the major peaks of the Southern Highlands. In season there are enormous blaeberries at the top.

Return to the quarry and follow the steep, rough path down. This incline was used by the railway that took the limestone down to kilns at the bottom, where it was turned into quicklime. Both red and grey squirrels live in the deciduous woods here. Cross a forest track and turn right **D** when the path meets a second track through mixed woodland, passing above the school used for outdoor pursuits. Finally, bear left off this track on to a path leading directly back to the Lodge. ●

Dunstaffnage Castle

Start	Ganavan Bay, 2 miles (3.2km) north of Oban
Distance	4 miles (6.4km)
Approximate time	2½ hours
Parking	Ganavan Bay car park
Refreshments	Pub and café at Ganavan
Ordnance Survey maps	Landranger 49 (Oban & East Mull) and Pathfinder 331, NM 83/93 (Oban & Loch Etive (West))

This is a lovely walk for a summer evening, with the sun sinking into an amber sea, and the mountains of Mull beyond. The one drawback to walking at that time is that you will find the castle closed to visitors. Both outward and return paths provide a succession of splendid viewpoints. There is one point on the lower route which requires agility in order to cross a gully.

Ganavan Bay is a sandy beach where there is every facility for a seaside holiday, as well as ample car parking. Pass through the gate at the north end of the beach, keeping dogs on leads. Already there are fine views seawards to Mull, Lismore and Morvern. The strange objects floating in the sea, looking like half-submerged pavilions,

are fish tanks belonging to the Fisheries Research Station at Dunbeg. Bear left on to the coastal path close to the shore, below the crags. Walking is not easy among the fallen boulders: take care not to sprain an ankle.

There is one point where something of a scramble is necessary to cross a gully **A**, but it should cause little trouble if you take the top way here rather than risking the jump over the crevasse on the lower one. Keep to the shoreline, ignoring a track going inland from a beach where stone has been removed for construction, to reach the sandy beach of Camas Rubha na Liathaig **B**. Skirt this to the rocky, scrubby promontory guarded by Dunstaffnage Castle. Dunbeg Marina can be seen ahead. Cross outflow pipes from the Fisheries Research Station

Dunstaffnage Castle

and follow the path through the trees to reach the shore again on the north-west side of the promontory. The castle **C** can now be seen on the right and is easily approached from this side.

Dunstaffnage was a stronghold of the MacDougalls, Lords of Lorn, and was successfully besieged in 1309 by King Robert the Bruce. He bestowed it on Arthur Campbell, one of his followers, and though it was subsequently passed back peacefully to the MacDougalls, in 1470, Dunstaffnage was later again granted to the Campbells, and the castle remained a Campbell residence until 1810 when it was burnt down. The walls, 11ft (3.3m) thick in places, follow the rocky platform on which the castle is built, which accounts for its very irregular shape. Considerable money has been spent recently on restoring this impressive fortress.

The chapel, hidden in woods a little to the west of the castle, is also worth visiting, with its gathering of Campbell tombs; from here it is easy to regain the coastal path and retrace steps to the western end of Camas Rubha na Liathaig **B**. Now make for a farm gate and cross the field beyond, keeping a low ridge to the right and the farm to the left. Go through another gate: here the path comes within yards of rejoining the shoreline path, but keep to the base of the crag, cross the stream and then take the steep grassy path up to the top of the cliff **D**. A little further on take the lower path following the fence. When this ends continue to another fence ahead which is crossed by a stile **E**. Another steep climb follows, and from the top the fish tanks can be seen again floating offshore. As the top of the ridge is reached a lovely view unfolds ahead – the islands of Mull and Kerrera looking particularly beautiful. From this vantage point the path descends to the shoreline path which takes you back to Ganavan Bay.

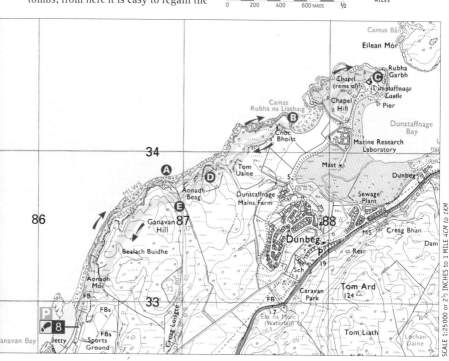

Dùn na Cuaiche, Inveraray

Start	Inveraray Castle
Distance	2½ miles (4km)
Approximate time	2 hours
Parking	Inveraray Castle
Refreshments	Tearoom at castle
Ordnance Survey maps	Landranger 56 (Loch Lomond & Inveraray), Pathfinders 367, NN 00/10 (Inveraray & Strachur) and 356, NN 01/11 (Glen Aray & Glen Shira)

Dùn na Cuaiche was strategically important to the Campbells, who could watch the mouths of three glens from the summit – Glen Fyne, Glen Aray and Glen Shira. Long before the coming of the Campbells, however, earlier settlers had recognised the height's defensive potential: there are remains of what may be Iron Age ramparts on the summit. In 1748 William Adam and Roger Morris erected the folly tower on Dùn na Cuaiche which adds to its picturesque appeal. The reward for the short climb (which is not for the faint-hearted or those not used to exercise) is a remarkable vista over Inveraray town and castle to mountains far distant.

Head north from the car park (the forecourt of the castle) past the monument which commemorates the execution of 17 Clan Campbell leaders by the 1st Marquis of Atholl in Inveraray in 1685. Cross the bridge and then bear half-right off the drive **A** on a path into the woods following the blue waymark. The lovely shady path soon emerges from the woods to cross another driveway and a meadow to a green gate on the far side (fasten this behind you). This leads into the arboretum which contains a host of specimen trees, many of them dating from the reign of Queen Victoria; some are even older.

The path now climbs past old kilns; these were built to provide lime to make the peaty soil of the Highlands less acidic and thus more fertile. 300 yds (274m) beyond these turn sharply to the right **B** on to a narrow path through the trees to reach a higher drive. Paths diverge at Post 8. Follow the blue waymark to climb up the steps to the left. The going is steep and the path narrow, often with a rope on the right-hand side to prevent unpleasant falls down precipitous slopes should one slip. Keep careful watch on children here.

A grand view is revealed as the path skirts a scree slope along a narrow ledge. Soon after this the narrow path joins with a wider one which continues to zigzag upwards, though in rather less spectacular style. There are now views to the north-west up Glen Aray. The folly tower **C** is revealed at the last moment. The views from here are truly magnificent and the exhausting climb is soon forgotten as one appreciates the scenery from this vantage point.

To return to the castle, retrace your steps down the carriageway to the point where it was joined by the footpath on the way up. However, do not turn right here but continue on the main track which twists down the hill on a comparatively gentle gradient. After passing Point 6 on the left **B** carry on to reach the arboretum and then the green gate on to the meadow. Continue to retrace your steps over the bridge to the castle, where refreshment is available from the tearoom in the holiday season. Alternative routes are offered in the excellent leaflet on the Dùn na Cuaiche Woodland Walks; this is obtainable from the castle kiosk when the castle is open, or at other times from the Estate Office or Tourist Information Centre. ●

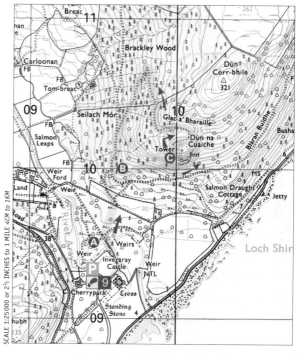

SCALE 1:25 000 or 2½ INCHES to 1 MILE 4CM to 1KM

Inveraray Castle and town from the Dùn na Cuaiche path

Creag Bhuidhe

Start	Killin
Distance	2½ miles (4km)
Approximate time	2 hours
Parking	Breadalbane Hall car park, Killin
Refreshments	Pubs and tearooms in Killin
Ordnance Survey maps	Landranger 51 (Loch Tay) and Pathfinder 334, NN 43/53 (Killin)

Sròn a' Chlachain is the summit which towers above Killin, though in fact the highest point of the hill lies behind: Creag Bhuidhe is 295ft (90m) higher. It is a wonderful viewpoint over Loch Tay and the mountains which stretch to the south and east. An adventurous route off the hill is suggested; this descends to the village by one of the old peat roads which were made centuries ago to give access to the diggings that once covered the hillside. Today trees cover the hill to the west of Killin and they (with bracken and other vegetation too) threaten to engulf the ancient track. For this reason the way down is difficult at times, but if the peat road is walked more frequently the path will become easier: it is a challenge worth accepting.

Walk past the northern (right-hand) side of Breadalbane Hall into the recreation park and make for the top where the swings and roundabouts are situated. Here there is a stile over the fence and a path through the meadow to the woods above. There is a bridge **Ⓐ** over the electric fence into the oak woods, where you may well see red squirrels. The path climbs steeply through the trees and soon emerges on to open hillside. It continues to climb relentlessly, in a westerly and then south-westerly direction. There is a fine view back over the town from underneath the electricity cables (photographers should

note that this walk is best undertaken in the afternoon).

A brief respite from steep climbing follows but the ascent soon resumes and is made worse by the number of false summits. There is a choice of two

Loch Tay from Creag Bhuidhe

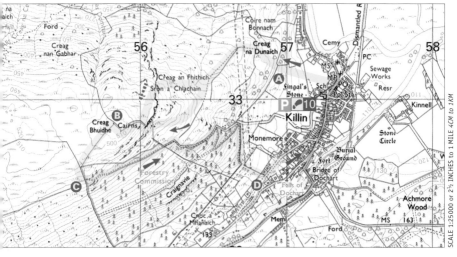

SCALE 1:25000 or 2½ INCHES to 1 MILE 4CM to 1KM

paths, and the easier way to tackle the last part is to climb up to Creag an Fhithich and then to walk south to the cairns on the two other summits, Sròn a' Chlachain and Creag Bhuidhe. The more direct route is steep but should present no problems apart from breathlessness. Bear right to approach the summit plateau from a bealach to avoid losing height.

It should take about an hour from the start to the summit **B**, the most westerly cairn. There are three large cairns altogether on the ridge, with a wall running east to west close by, which must have provided material for their construction – they are very handsome. From the summit cairn it is easy to see the sparkling water of Lochan Lairig Cheile in Glen Ogle which lies due south.

The return to Killin is via one of the old peat roads which are a feature of this hill. (Note that the route suggested by a Tourist Office leaflet, descending north into Glen Lochay, is no longer practicable because of an electric fence). From the summit cairn head south-west, descending so that the forest comes into view. Head to the right of

the trees keeping on the crest of low crags, descending to the deer fence when these end. Go through the deer fence at the corner, and then walk down alongside it (with trees on the left) to a stile about 100 yds (90m) lower down **C**. This signals the beginning of the ancient peat road which curves around the hillside near the top of the forestry planting, heading towards Loch Tay. Take care to avoid the deep runnels which follow the path.

At the eastern end of the forest the old road burrows down through the conifers, and has become very moist and overhung in places. Its steep banks are still obvious and it is still possible to visualise the ponies, laden with panniers, which used to bring their loads of fuel back to the village from the peat diggings. In some places the track is becoming choked with bracken, but the passage of more walkers should help in keeping it clear.

The track seems to end at the bottom of the wood by a pylon. Cross the fence (the stile which was once here appears to have vanished) and descend through the meadow to a gate directly below by a sheepfold and a white bungalow. Pass through the gate and then turn left on to Manse Road just below **D** to walk back into the village. ●

Ben A'an

Start	200 yds (182m) west of Trossachs Hotel
Distance	2 miles (3.2km)
Approximate time	1½ hours
Parking	Car park on south side of A821 opposite start
Refreshments	Pub, hotels and tearooms near start
Ordnance Survey maps	Landranger 57 (Stirling & The Trossachs) and Explorer 11 (The Trossachs)

The view from the summit of Ben A'an is out of all proportion to the modest height of the hill (1512ft/461m). It serves as an excellent introduction to the geography of the area, and as a test of stamina to show how fit you are before you tackle the more demanding routes which follow.

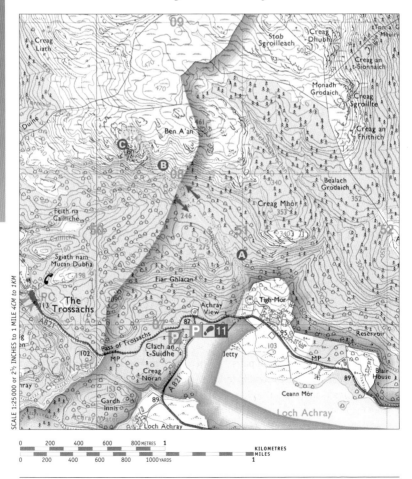

Loch Katrine from Ben A'an

Cross the road from the car park to reach a path which climbs up steeply through mixed woodland and is soon accompanied by a burn on the right. The path levels out soon after crossing the burn by a footbridge Ⓐ. On the left there is a viewpoint. The path meanders through pines and when it emerges from the trees the conical summit of Ben A'an is suddenly revealed ahead. The path now becomes more demanding, a steep scramble up rock that is loosened by thousands of pairs of feet each year. Pause occasionally to catch your breath and enjoy the view looking back.

The climbers' route leaves to the left Ⓑ, while the 'tourist' path continues to the top. It generally takes about an hour to reach the summit though the super-fit can do it in half this time. The highest point on the route Ⓒ is 1491ft (454m) and the path ends at its twin rocky knolls each providing vistas in different directions – west over Loch Katrine and south-east over Loch Achray. Twice a day in summer the sound of a pipe band will drift up from the steamer *The Lady of the Lake* as she leaves for trips up Loch Katrine. The summit of Ben Venue looks very formidable on the other side of the water. An underground aqueduct beneath Ben A'an takes water from the Glen Finglas Reservoir to replenish Loch Katrine, which serves Glasgow and its area.

The return is by the same path and should not take much more than 30 minutes.

Bracklinn Falls and Callander Craig

Start	Callander
Distance	4 miles (6.4km)
Approximate time	2 hours
Parking	Bracklinn Falls car park, Bracklinn Road
Refreshments	Pubs and cafés in Callander
Ordnance Survey maps	Landranger 57 (Stirling & The Trossachs) and Explorer 11 (The Trossachs)

This route offers an unusual mixture, in this area, of woodland, pastoral, and crag-top walking, and includes a visit to a waterfall which is always spectacular after heavy rain. Callander stands at the gateway to the Trossachs, and from its Craig which overlooks the town on its north-western side there are good views of the Highlands to the north and west, as well as over the level plain eastwards towards Doune and Stirling. This route is not suitable for walkers with dogs.

Descend the steps from the car park and turn left along the path to the Falls. At first the view to the right is screened by conifers, but it soon opens up and the main road can be seen crossing the level plain towards Doune. Pass through a kissing-gate and descend to the Falls **A**, crossing them by the sturdy footbridge, a successor to the ramshackle wooden one which Sir Walter Scott recklessly rode across for a wager. Bear right on to a path which follows the top of the gorge (take heed of the 'No dogs' notice) and make for the top of the woods, following the wall there to an iron kissing-gate **B**.

Go through this and climb up with the fence to the right of a gate **C** before a cattleshed. (Note that a detour to the left of the wall may be necessary during the lambing season.) Go through the gate on to a pleasant grassy track which

curves around the flank of the hill. Ben Ledi is well seen to the west, though Callander is hidden. The track passes through a gate into a forest and has been resurfaced for much of its course through this. Tree-growth allows only rare glimpses of the scenery over Brackland Glen, but a track entering from the right heralds the end of this section and soon afterwards it descends to cross Keltie Water **D**. There is another grand waterfall and rock pool below the bridge here.

Climb the stile on the other side of the bridge and walk up the track to the made-up road: turn left and walk along it for nearly a mile (1.6km). At the apex of a long hairpin bend **E** look for a path on the right waymarked to Callander Crags. This zigzags steeply up the hill through scrubby woodland to reach the ridge, at the top of which is

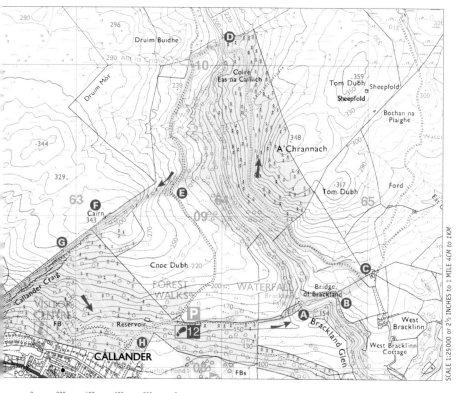

SCALE 1:25000 or 2½ INCHES to 1 MILE 4CM to 1KM

0	200	400	600	800 METRES	1
					KILOMETRES
					MILES
0	200	400	600 YARDS	½	

the cairn **F** built to commemorate Queen Victoria's Jubilee. This is a fine viewpoint for many hills covered in this book, with Ben Ledi on the left of an arc which ends with the twin peaks of Ben Vorlich and Stuc a' Chroin on the right. To the south-east are the two landmarks of Stirling (the castle and the Wallace Monument) with the Ochil Hills beyond, while southwards the Campsie Hills lie on the far side of the Forth Valley.

The path begins to descend after the cairn, and immediately after a small bridge **G** turn left off the main path to walk down steps which zigzag between the thickly planted trees. Altogether

there are 389 steps to descend before the path comes to a new forest track. Turn left on to this track and then left again when it meets the road **H**, which climbs back up to the car park where the walk began. ●

Callander, the gateway to the Trossachs, is overlooked by Ben Ledi

Ardcastle Wood

Start	Ardcastle Wood, 2 miles (3.25km) north of Lochgair on the north-west shore of Loch Fyne
Distance	5 miles (8km)
Approximate time	3 hours
Parking	Forestry picnic area off A83 2 miles (3.2km) north of Lochgair
Refreshments	Hotel at Lochgair
Ordnance Survey maps	Landranger 55 (Lochgilphead) and Pathfinder 378, NR 99 (Minard)

This must be one of the very best of all Forestry Commission walks. Although forestry tracks are used for some of the way they never seem tedious and the pines are particularly fragrant. But the main feature of the route is the long stretch beside a seldom-visited part of the Loch Fyne shoreline. Wildlife abounds here – you will see a range of birds from goldcrests to waders, and might even encounter an otter. As you will see from the Forestry map at the start of the walk, the blue and white routes are short-cuts; however, the odds are that you will not be inclined to use them.

There is a good viewpoint at the car park, overlooking Loch Gair and Loch Fyne. Leave the car park and take the forestry road on the right, following the yellow waymarks and thus bearing right at the first junction. The fine hills on the left surround Lochan Dubh to the east of Loch Glashan. Bear left at the

Loch Fyne from Ardcastle Wood

next junction. The red route leaves to the right **A** to climb to a viewpoint, and soon afterwards the route described here also branches right on to a grassy track which wends its way down to the lochside, following the right bank of a burn which reaches the shore by flowing down a small waterfall on to the beach **B**.

It only takes 20 minutes to reach this beauty-spot, ideal for a picnic at the purpose-built table overlooking the loch. The path south follows close to the shore, birches, foxgloves and yellow irises providing foregrounds for panoramas of water and mountain. When the path joins with a track, walking remains a pleasure, the pines being exceptionally resinous. A small bay is skirted before the blue route, the first Forestry Commission short cut,

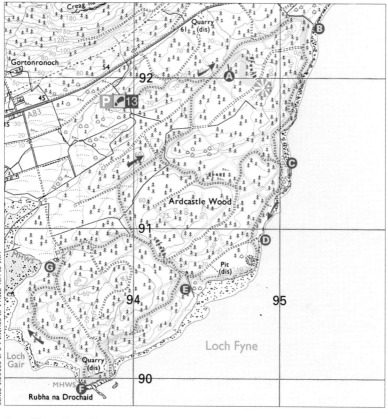

SCALE 1:25 000 or 2½ INCHES to 1 MILE 4CM to 1KM

leaves inland **C**. The track enters tall stands of timber which screen views of Loch Fyne, and a minor track branches to the left **D** to another picnic-place sited on a rocky promontory overlooking a beach. From here walk down to the sand quarry which is a habitat of shy lizards (and possibly snakes as well).

Another forest track is reached on the other side of the quarry, and as this begins to climb the white route leaves to return to the car park **E**. The longer route bears to the left and continues climbing; there is a pair of well-sited seats at the top and fine views up and down the loch. The removal of timber from these slopes has left bleached, skeletal branches, but in compensation there is a splendid display of foxgloves in early summer. A rough, embanked path descends to an old quarry and then rounds Rubha na Drochaid to reach another picnic-place **F**. The writer has watched otters from here as they scrambled over rocks and swam in Loch Gair, a lagoon which looks as though it belongs to the South Seas rather than the Highlands.

The path now rejoins a forest track to begin the return. Abundant thistles here provide goldcrests with a feast of seeds and they will feed greedily as humans walk by. Look for a mown path on the left which goes to St Bride's graveyard and ruined chapel **G** – a lovely place to rest, briefly or eternally.

One by one the short cuts rejoin the return route, which follows the main forest track. The walking now is less interesting, and it may come as a relief for hot feet to make the last turn to the left which leads back to the car park. ●

Isle of Kerrera

Start	Kerrera Jetty
Distance	6 miles (9.7km)
Approximate time	3½ hours
Parking	Kerrera Ferry slipway, Gallanach road, 2 miles (3.2km) south-west of Oban
Refreshments	None
Ordnance Survey maps	Landranger 49 (Oban & East Mull), Pathfinders 343, NM 62/72 (Firth of Lorn North) and 344, NM 82/92 (Oban South & Kilninver)

The earliest ferry to the isle of Kerrera departs on the dot of nine o'clock in season and the next is at 10.30am. Thereafter there is a regular service (every hour or so), with intending passengers being asked to turn a board to show the ferryman that he is in fact wanted at the advertised times (in any event it would be as well to check with Oban Tourist Information Centre first – see the list of useful organisations on page 94). Kerrera has the air of romance about it common to all the islands off this coast. It is an intensely beautiful place, well worth the small effort involved in getting there.

On landing turn left at the telephone box along the track which follows the eastern shore of the island. There are lovely coastal views across the Horse Shoe to the Sound of Kerrera and the mainland beyond. The track goes through a gate before the first farm (Ardchoirc): fork left here to continue along the coast. The field on the left is called Dail Righ, the 'King's Field', where Alexander II of Scotland died in 1249. The crofts of Gallanach are well seen on the other side of the Sound, below steep crags, while Oban is to the north-east.

The Little Horse Shoe is a tiny bay which appears to be a graveyard of fishing boats. The track passes in front of the lovely whitewashed cottages overlooking the bay, which is sheltered

by a steep, tree-covered hill. The track continues, snaking uphill to lose the view of the sea, though mainland peaks are just visible to the south-east.

Fork to the left **Ⓐ** before the white cottage (Upper Gylen), going through a gate by a sheepfold to climb the hill in front of the cottage, with a wall to the right. After a very short distance a wonderful view is revealed below – the ruins of Gylen Castle **Ⓑ** provide an atmospheric foreground to the prospect of the Firth of Lorn. The castle had a short history, being built in 1582 by the MacDougalls of Dunollie and lasting only until 1647 when it was left a ruin by Covenanters.

From the castle follow the cliffs west, crossing a stream and taking a path at the foot of a steep crag to turn north.

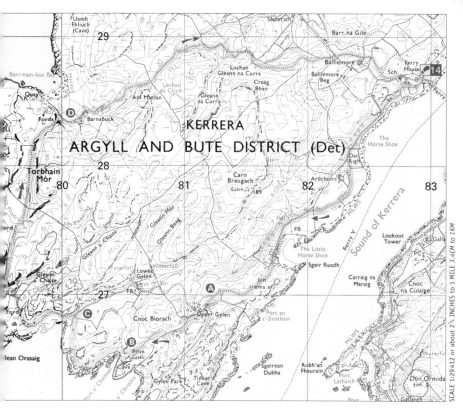

SCALE 1:29412 or about 2¼ INCHES to 1 MILE 3.4CM to 1KM

```
0    200   400   600   800 METRES  1
                                   KILOMETRES
                                   MILES
0    200   400   600 YARDS  ½
```

This path joins a track **C** on to which you turn left to pass two cottages, the second one (Ardmore) derelict. The narrow path which is followed uphill from the remains of the second cottage was once a drove road. Cattle from Mull were landed on Kerrera at Barr-nam-boc Bay and driven south to be shipped to the mainland from the tiny haven of Port Dubh. (Alternatively they would be swum to the mainland from the east coast of the island.)

The Sound of Kerrera from the Little Horse Shoe

Level ground is soon reached above Ardmore and the views to Mull and Lismore improve as the path heads northwards. Morvern lies beyond the lighthouse on Lismore.

The going is easy on this smooth grassy path, which descends to another deserted croft – Barnabuck **D**. Presumably it is the shelter offered by Mull which allows trees (sycamore and ash) to grow in this enchantingly beautiful spot.

Take the zigzag track up the hill from Barnabuck. There is a fine view when the crest of the hill is reached, and Oban will soon be seen ahead, with the distinctive shape of Ben Cruachan in the distance (on a clear day you will see Ben Nevis too). When the track meets with the one from Slaterich turn right to return to the ferry. ●

The Ancient Forest below Beinn Dubhchraig

Start	Near Tyndrum
Distance	6½ miles (10.5km)
Approximate time	4 hours
Parking	Look for sign to Dalrigh and Arach on south side of A82 about 1½ miles (2.4km) south-east of Tyndrum. Park on disused loop of old road
Refreshments	Pub and restaurant at Tyndrum
Ordnance Survey maps	Landranger 50 (Glen Orchy) and Outdoor Leisure 38 (Ben Nevis & Glen Coe)

Many approaches to the major peaks of the Southern Highlands are delightful walks in themselves. This route, which gives access to Beinn Dubhchraig, passes through a particularly beautiful remnant of the ancient Caledonian pine forest which once covered much of the Highlands. The return is made through modern plantings of conifers, a part of the walk which is far from boring since for most of the way there are splendid all-round views of the hills around Strath Fillan. Note that at the forest edge on the return leg of the walk after **C** is a 6ft (2m)-high deergate which is sometimes locked. However, the landowners have no objection to people climbing over it and this should present no problem for most walkers.

Walk down the old road to the bridge over the River Cononish, crossing the West Highland Way just before the bridge. After the bridge turn right up a track which follows the railway line westwards, crossing it about a mile (1.6km) from the river. Continue on the track for about 250 yds (225m) and just where this levels **A** look for a faint footpath on the right, which leads down a bank and across flat ground to a bridge over the Allt Gleann Auchreoch. Turn left after the bridge following a lovely path by the burn which climbs through splendid trees, many of them

Scots pines which once formed the ancient Caledonian Forest. There are also fine birches, rowans and oaks.

The path climbs steeply around a beautiful waterfall which drops into a deep, tree-fringed pool. Cross two deer fences, about ¼ mile (400m) apart, by tall ladders. There follows an energetic ascent over open ground on a clear path – there are more waterfalls on the left and the view back is superb. Look for a solitary birch tree standing by a waterfall, cross the stream close to this point **B** and climb the slope on the other side to reach the start (or end) of a

SCALE 1:25 000 or 2½ INCHES to 1 MILE 4CM to 1KM

| 0 | 200 | 400 | 600 | 800 METRES | 1 |
| 0 | 200 | 400 | 600 YARDS | ½ | KILOMETRES MILES |

forestry track. The planting here is comparatively recent and when the trees grow they will probably hide the wonderful view, a grand panorama of the mountains to the east. Remarkably, two railways run up Strath Fillan, one on each side of the valley. On the other side of Gleann Auchreoch can be seen the track which is the final part of the

walk. It takes some time to reach this – the stream must be crossed first, and then there is a short climb to reach the track heading northwards **C**.

There is more fine mountain scenery to enjoy on the final section: Beinn Odhar is the distinctive conical hill to the north of Tyndrum. The track steadily descends to reach the bridge over the railway again, and from here the outward route is simply reversed to the River Cononish and main road. ●

Ben Venue

Start	Loch Achray Hotel
Distance	6 miles (9.7km)
Approximate time	4 hours
Parking	On track behind Loch Achray Hotel or in parking area ½ mile (800m) north of hotel
Refreshments	Loch Achray Hotel
Ordnance Survey maps	Landranger 57 (Stirling & The Trossachs) and Explorer 11 (The Trossachs)

Although Ben Venue's height (2391ft/727m) puts it somewhat below the status of a Corbett, it demands respect as a rugged little hill, while its position overlooking Lochs Katrine and Achray makes it a key viewpoint for all of the Trossachs and much of the countryside beyond. Sir Walter Scott wrote of 'huge

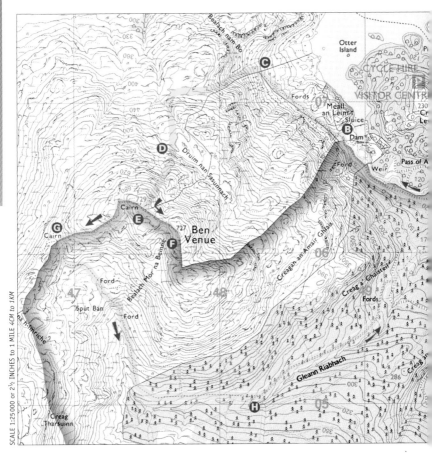

SCALE 1:25000 or 2½ INCHES to 1 MILE 4CM to 1KM

Benvenue' in The Lady of the Lake *and* Rob Roy, *and the exploits of the latter renegade chieftain are given some historical muscle by the fact that the Bealach nam Bo, a secret rocky defile on the flank of the hill above Loch Katrine, was used by Highlanders when they drove stolen cattle to their home glens after sorties into the lowlands. Note that the return leg of this route, through the forest, is likely to be very muddy.*

Take the forestry track at the rear of the Loch Achray Hotel and bear right when this forks **A** (waymarked routes go to the left). Ben Venue (its name means 'mountain of the caves') looks a challenge as the track winds down through the forest with Achray Water to

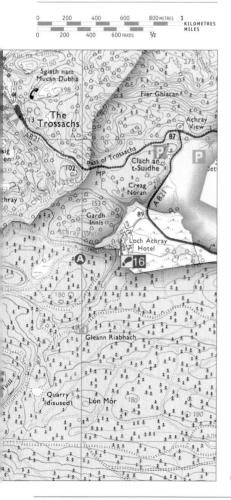

the right. At the end of the forestry track there are steps over the fence and the path then goes past the sluices before coming to another fence and a sheepfold **B**. Cross this to follow a distinct path with a burn on the right.

The path emerges on to open hillside giving a beautiful vista over Loch Katrine: craggy Ben A'an is clearly seen across the water, an outlier of Meall Reamhar and Meall Gainmheich. The path ends at a new fence crossed by a stile **C**. The route described here assaults the hill directly by following this fence up the steep north-eastern slopes; those wishing an easier alternative would continue through the Bealach nam Bo (which is facing you at this point) before swinging south to tackle the less steep northern face. In both cases paths are either very faint or non-existent.

If you decide to follow the direct route turn left and climb up with old fence posts to the left. There are signs of a rudimentary path through the heather and blaeberries at first, but this fades as height is gained. The slope is arduous but in recompense there are wonderful views back which will be a good excuse to catch breath. Try to keep the fence posts in sight as you climb, though owing to the nature of the ground they will tend to be further away to the left as you get higher. To the right there are impressive rocky knolls. The ascent eases briefly at Druim nan Sasunnach **D** (the name means 'ridge of the

Sassenach' – what was he doing up here?) which is a broad level area at the head of a small burn. At this point head towards a notch in the hill on the skyline to come close to the fence posts again. The steamer on Loch Katrine looks a toy now, and people promenading along the loch shore can only just be seen.

A steep gully soon has to be crossed, and after this climb up directly to the ridge **E** of Ben Venue and turn left to reach the summit **F**.

All of the major heights of the Southern Highlands can be identified from here in a wonderful panorama which extends far to the south as well. The return is made by walking back past the point **E** where the ridge was gained to reach a cairn. From here walk south-westwards to a second cairn **G** which is where the descent begins. A well-used path drops down to the forest from here, heading south. It follows old fencing posts and is an easy route to follow to reach the trees below.

Once in the forest the way veers eastwards, entering a wide firebreak at first. This path may be boggy in places. After about $\frac{1}{2}$ mile (800m) the path becomes a forest track **H**. Follow this for just over $\frac{1}{2}$ mile (800m) until you reach a crossroads of tracks. Go straight ahead here, following a stream which runs along on the right-hand side. This path is less well-defined and may be very boggy. After another $\frac{1}{4}$ mile (400m), keep straight on at another intersection of tracks, following green- and brown-topped posts. Soon the original track from the Loch Achray hotel is rejoined, and welcome refreshments are in prospect as you return to the starting point. ●

Loch Katrine from Ben Venue

Doune Hill

Start	Glenmollochan, at head of Glen Luss
Distance	7½ miles (12.1km)
Approximate time	5 hours
Parking	Very limited parking at Glenmollochan
Refreshments	None
Ordnance Survey maps	Landranger 56 (Loch Lomond & Inveraray) and Outdoor Leisure 39 (Loch Lomond)

Although Doune Hill is officially 100ft or so below being a Corbett, its ascent, with that of Beinn Eich, makes an invigorating day out. Few summits achieve such a superlative 360° view, and after the usual initial hard slog of an hour or so the going is easy. Hills like this (its top is at 2408ft/734m) are not to be despised and climbing this one will make the walker look forward to more days on the Luss hills. This is very much a hill for sheep, and dogs are unwelcome.

There are only about five or six parking spaces at Glenmollochan in Glen Luss, and if these are already occupied the only alternative is to use the car park in Luss village and stride the 2½ miles (4km) up the glen. From Glenmollochan go up the lane to Edentaggart, taking in the view up Glen Mollochan at the second bridge.

After the farm (its yard can be bypassed through a sheepfold) continue up the track and pass through the gate. Here there is also a gate on the right **A** which gives access to the lower slopes of Beinn Eich. Go through this and climb up with the wall to the right; as you climb note the fine corrie (Coire Cann) on the other side of Glen Luss and the view of Loch Lomond which opens up to the east. Another gate ahead gives access to the open hill through a sheep fence. Continue to climb directly up to reach the ridge leading to the summit of Beinn Eich **B** (you will find several false summits *en route*). The path to this first objective runs on the top of a rocky causeway (with a low cliff to the left).

Doune Hill

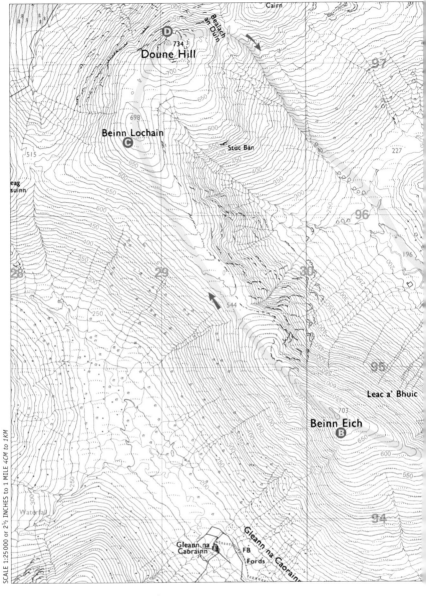

Beinn Lochain

Doune Hill

Beinn Eich

Stuc Bàn

Leac a' Bhuic

Gleann na Caorainn

Gleann na Caorainn

Waterfall

Fords

FB

SCALE 1:25 000 or 2½ INCHES to 1 MILE *4CM to 1KM*

Ben Lomond is well seen from here, as is the Cobbler. The summit proves to be a very narrow ridge with precipitous views down the glens on each side. The square-topped hill ahead is Cruach an t-Sidhein, though the ridge bends to the right of this towards Doune Hill. Peat banks are frequent obstacles before the start of the climb up Beinn Lochain.

Another short descent follows after you reach the summit **C**. Now Loch Long can be seen beyond Glen Douglas, as can the summits of the Arrochar Alps. The short ascent to the triangulation pillar on Doune Hill **D** seems effortless after what has gone before. Few hills of such modest height can boast such a superb all-round view.

Climb down eastwards from the summit, taking care as the ground is steep and rough in places. The unnamed

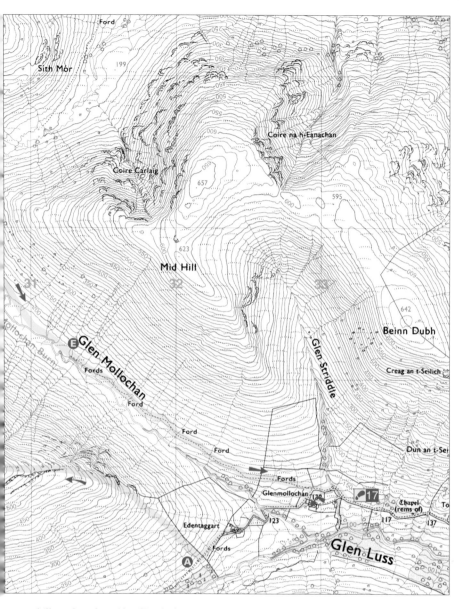

hill on the other side of Bealach an Duin looks a promising viewpoint but offers little that cannot be seen from Doune Hill. The bealach is criss-crossed by the tyre-marks of shepherds' trial bikes; follow the headwaters of the Mollochan Burn down to the glen. The way down is steep and tussocky and lacks an obvious path although old fencing posts to the right of the burn may be useful as rough guides. In spring and summer a wealth of wild flowers adorn the lower parts of the valley, amongst them several species of orchid.

At the bottom of the glen there is the vestige of a path in places but the way close to the burn is quite wet and difficult, and it is probably easiest to walk a little above the stream on the drier, north-eastern side of the glen. The Land Rover track begins (or ends) at what looks like the remains of a bothy **E**, and leads to the lane just above Glenmollochan, the starting point. ●

Ben Ledi

Start	Corriechrombie bridge, 3 miles (4.8km) west of Callander
Distance	6 miles (9.7km)
Approximate time	3½ hours
Parking	Forestry Commission Ben Ledi car park ½ mile (800m) north of Falls of Leny car park but on western side of A84 (look for sign to Strathyre Forest Cabins)
Refreshments	Pubs and tearoom at Strathyre
Ordnance Survey maps	Landranger 57 (Stirling & The Trossachs) and Explorer 11 (The Trossachs)

Although at 2883ft (879m) Ben Ledi does not attain Munro status, it is the highest summit of the Trossachs and is visible from many places to the east. It dominates Callander, is well seen from Stirling and can even be identified from the Cheviots on an exceptionally clear day. The route described here climbs up by picturesque Stank Glen and then strikes west to reach the ridge at Bealach nan Corp. The summit lies about a mile to the south. Note that it would be unwise to attempt this route unless the weather is set fair.

Do not take the path to Ben Ledi which begins at the parking place but instead walk northwards along the track on the west bank of the River Leny – in Gaelic the *Garbh Uisge* (the old trackbed of the railway runs parallel to this on the right and this is a popular route for cyclists). After a handful of cottages the lane becomes a forestry track and begins to climb. Ardnandave Hill is the impressive summit which is visible ahead at this point.

Take the left fork just after the track swings away from the old railway, and at the first sharp bend in this track Ⓐ a footpath (marked by a white and green waymark painted on a rock) goes into the trees straight ahead. This climbs directly to another track. The path continues to the right of the hairpin

bend here to reach a third track with a burn close by, which you cross Ⓑ to a path opposite marked by a white post. This is steep but the walking very pleasant by the side of the stream.

The path emerges from the forest into a perfect Highland glen Ⓒ. The direct way to the summit is to climb up the very steep slope on the left following the edge of the trees. This is a rugged and exhausting route. The one suggested here lies more to the right (north-westwards) where the gradient is less severe and there are still waymarks (yellow ones) to guide you. The path enters the forest again briefly and climbs on the left side of a burn to reach open hillside. Turn left at a yellow and green waymark to pass through a few more trees, then follow the path up

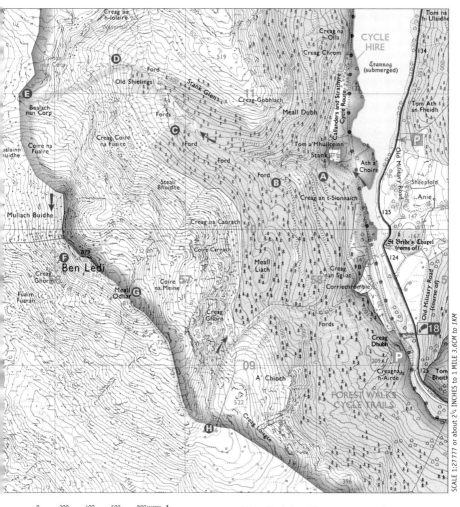

SCALE 1:27777 or about 2¼ INCHES to 1 MILE 3.6CM to 1KM

0	200	400	600	800 METRES	1	
						KILOMETRES
						MILES
0	200	400	600 YARDS	½		

the open hillside again to reach the fence. The waymarking ends here **D**.

Cross the stile and continue to climb towards the ridge. This part seems endless but at last broken fence posts can be seen marking the crest. This is the Bealach nan Corp **E** which takes its name from the Lochan nan Corp a short distance to the north of this route. A funeral party from the glens to the west, travelling in winter to St Brides Chapel on the bank of the River Leny, once foolishly attempted to cross this tiny loch, but the ice broke and corpse and mourners were all lost.

The climb is still strenuous as the fence posts are followed southwards. Glen Finglas Reservoir can be seen on the right and Loch Lubnaig to the left. The final ½ mile (800m) is on top of the ridge on springy grass and makes the exertion of the ascent seem a small price to pay for the view, which is even better from the summit **F** with its triangulation pillar. Just beyond this point there is a large cairn bearing a cross made of old fence posts. It should have taken you about two hours to reach this point.

The way down follows the conventional summit path, still keeping close to the old fence posts to reach the cairn on Meall Odhar **G**. Loch

Venachar and the Lake of Menteith can be seen ahead. The path bends sharply to the left ⒣ (away from the fence posts) before meeting a Land Rover track. The forest serves as a lovely foreground to views of Loch Lubnaig.

Cross the fence into the forest and follow the well-maintained path down. Duck-boarding is used to take the path over boggy areas eroded by the passing of too many boot-clad feet. Although the descent is steep the numerous burns which accompany it provide welcome refreshment as they tumble over nearby rocks. The path ends at the Ben Ledi car park at the bridge over the Leny. ●

Ben Ledi from Stank Glen

Conic Hill and Balmaha

Start	Where West Highland Way crosses the Drymen–Gartmore road
Distance	9½ miles (15.3km)
Approximate time	4½ hours
Parking	Forestry Commission car park on Drymen – Gartmore road 1½ miles (2.4km) north of Drymen
Refreshments	Pub and tearoom at Balmaha
Ordnance Survey maps	Landrangers 56 (Loch Lomond & Inveraray) and 57 (Stirling & The Trossachs) and Outdoor Leisure 39 (Loch Lomond)

Prospective long-distance walkers can get a flavour of the West Highland Way from this route, which passes through forest and across open moorland before climbing steeply around the flank of Conic Hill (1174ft/358m), a magnificent viewpoint at the southern end of Loch Lomond. Balmaha is always busy with visitors in summer, and walkers enjoying a well-earned pint at the pub may well be serenaded by a piper. A direct return is made along the main road as far as Milton (there is a wide footpath) before a farm track leads off back to the forest. There is a 'No dogs' notice at the point where the Way leaves the forest for the open hill.

Take the track into the forest; this is an early part of the West Highland Way. Initially there are views towards Loch Lomond but these are soon blocked off by trees. It is easy walking on a good track. Do not take the alternative route to the left offered by a waymark after about 2 miles (3.2km) **A** but carry straight on along the West Highland Way. The track becomes more tortuous and is lined by bluebells ('hyacinths' in Scotland, where 'bluebell' means the English harebell) and primroses in late spring. The forest road ends and the Way becomes a metalled path which leads through a camp site dedicated to backpackers. At the end of the forest there are high steps over the deer fence

B. Excellent walking follows over open moorland. The path ahead can be clearly seen climbing the eastern flank of Conic Hill. Beinn Bhreac is the greater height to the right. The path drops down to cross two sparkling burns, the first being a lovely spot to picnic, with the cool water soothing hot feet. It will be just as well to take advantage of this, as the hardest part of the walk follows.

This is the steep climb up the twisting path on the northern side of Conic Hill, which lies directly on the course of the Highland Boundary Fault (see Walk 7). It is some consolation to know that the ascent in the other direction is even steeper. Pause occasionally to enjoy the view. Ben Lomond is slowly revealed ahead, and then, as the ascent eases, Loch Lomond too comes into view. This is one of the best places for an overall view of the loch. An even wider view can be obtained from the summit of the hill, which is easily reached by paths leaving to the left. Beware of being startled here by the sudden whoosh of a passing hang-glider: they may occasionally provide photographers with unusual foreground interest in this grandest of panoramas.

The path descends steeply through Bealach Ard **C**. Deep steps make the way down awkward but safe. The path

threads through a resinous pine wood with ancient Scots pines at the top. Turn right when the path meets with a forest track **D**; in spring look to the right to view great expanses of bluebells (hyacinths!) before the track reaches the car park at Balmaha.

On warm days many walkers take the opportunity to bathe in the loch here, but alternative refreshment is available in the pub just to the right (west) of the car park.

Turn left along the main road to resume the walk. There is a wide footpath alongside the busy road and this is followed for about an hour into the tidy village of Milton of Buchanan. Here there is a white church, village hall, school and cottages. Cross the

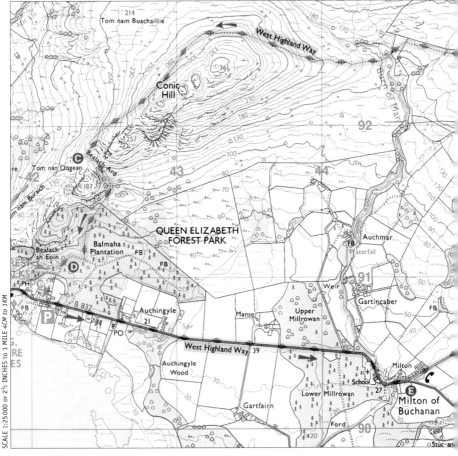

bridge to the telephone box where the route turns to the left **E** to follow a sandy track uphill. This passes the handsome farmhouse of Creityhall on the left and then continues to climb to reach the forest. There are more views to Loch Lomond on the left. When the track joins with the West Highland Way again **A** (at the waymark mentioned earlier denoting an alternative route) turn right to retrace steps through the forest to the starting point. ●

Loch Lomond from Conic Hill

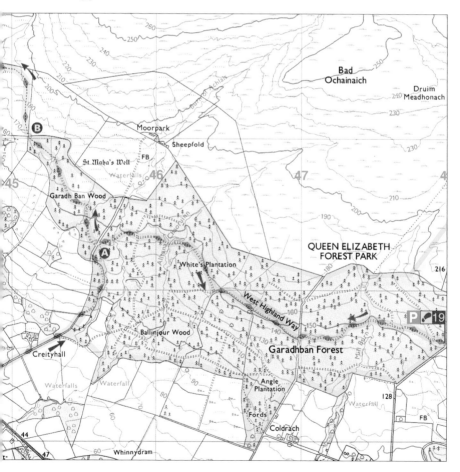

Glen Finglas

Start	Brig o' Turk
Distance	13½ miles (21.5km)
Approximate time	5½ hours
Parking	Turn off A821 into village and drive past school to where road forks and there are hydro notices forbidding further vehicular access. There is space for off-road parking here
Refreshments	Pub and restaurant at Brig o'Turk
Ordnance Survey maps	Landranger 57 (Stirling & The Trossachs), Explorer 11 (The Trossachs)

This long walk passes through the wild upper reaches of Glen Finglas, climbing to the 2000-ft (600m) contour before beginning a return leg down the equally unfrequented Gleann nam Meann. There is a good track all the way, and it would be quite hard to get lost even in poor visibility if this is followed. The circuit is a favourite with off-road cyclists who, though they will hardly catch walkers on the way up, may surprise them as they speed down. Look for stags on the skyline as you walk below the crags of Coire Ceothach and Carn Dubh. To check on access during the stalking season telephone 01877 376256.

From the end of the public road take the right fork, following the public footpath sign ('Balquhidder 10 miles'). The road climbs up steeply, accompanied by the sound of rushing water from the left. Soon the concrete dam can be seen through the trees, and after half an hour's walking the track emerges into open country and there is a splendid view of the Glen Finglas Reservoir as well as a sobering one of the track winding up into the mountains far beyond its head. As you walk up beside the reservoir beyond the farm (where the surfaced road ends) the route to be followed looks even more daunting. In a year of drought when the water in the reservoir is low the small island at its southern end resembles the

top of a coconut. Ben Ledi is well seen to the right.

After about an hour the track divides **A**, a mile (1.6km) or so from the head of the reservoir. Keep to the track following its shore, crossing the bridge over Allt Gleann nam Meann. Tom an Fhaile, with its crown of trees, is no longer an island after a succession of dry years.

At the top of the reservoir the track descends steeply – a brief respite before a long, unrelenting climb. There are plenty of trees in the glen at first but gradually these thin out as height is gained. Soon the reservoir is hidden

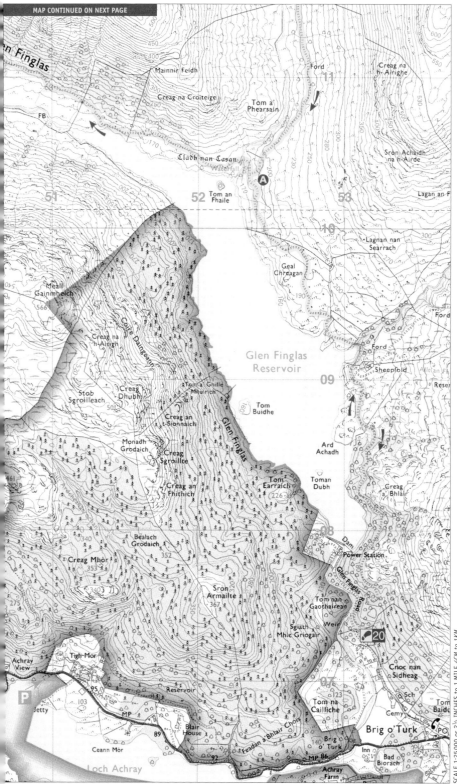

SCALE 1:25000 or 2½ INCHES to 1 MILE 4CM to 1KM

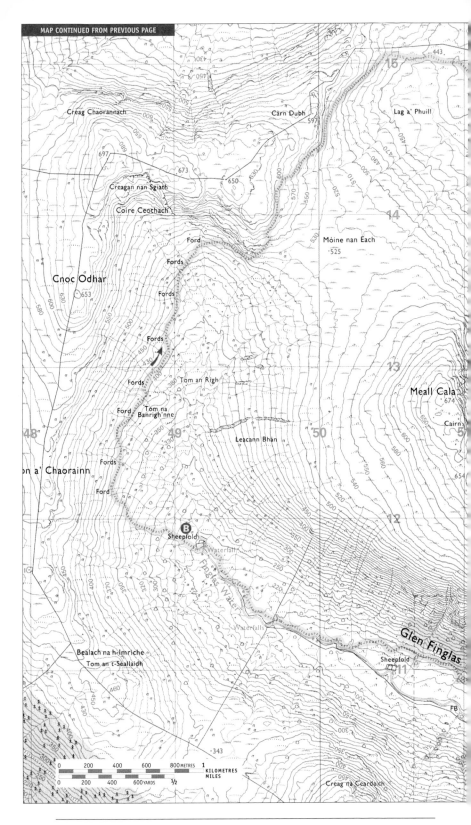

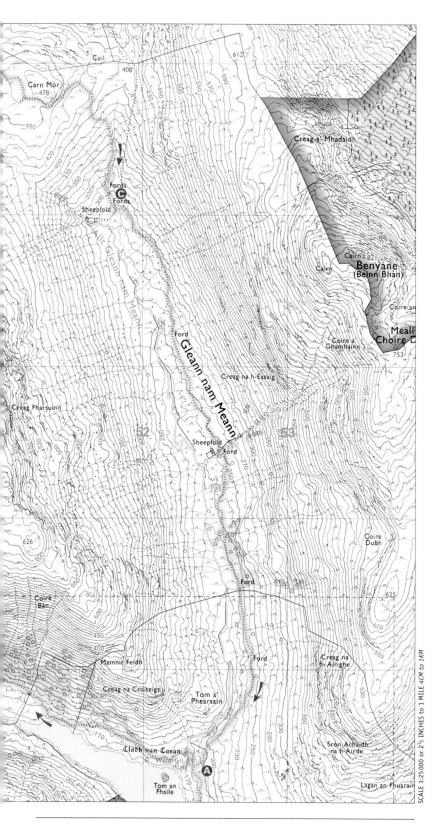

Cuil

Carn Mór
·478·

Creag a Mhadaidh

Fords
Fords
Sheepfold

Allt Gleann nam Meann

Cairn 821
Benyane
(Beinn Bhàn)
Cairn

Coire an

Meall
Choire D

Ford

Gleann nam Meann

Coire a
Ghamhainn

Creag na h-Easaig

Creag Fharsuinn

52

53

Sheepfold   Ford

Coire
Dubh

626

Ford

625

Coire
Bàn

Coire
Dubh

Mainnir Feidh

Ford

Creag na
h-Airighe

Creag na Croiteige

Tom a'
Phearsain

Cladh nan Casan
Waterfall

A

Sròn Achaidh
na h-Airde

Tom an
Fhaile

Lagan an Fhuarain

SCALE 1:25000 or 2½ INCHES to 1 MILE 4CM to 1KM

from view, though Ben Ledi still overlooks the glen.

After approximately three hours' walking (after a ford and sheepfold) **B** the track leaves Finglas Water and begins to climb more seriously (in compensation the reservoir is in view again to the south-east, and the track can be clearly seen ahead climbing up the flank of the hill towards the skyline). Small birch trees manage to survive here, almost at the top of the glen. Deer on the crest of the hills above the track look down without interest on walkers struggling towards the col between the two glens. Even at this height there are many refreshing burns.

The head of the pass is at last reached beyond Carn Dubh, and Benvane can be seen ahead as the track swings eastwards. A little further and Gleann nam Meann is revealed with the track clearly visible below, running southwards. The footpath from Balquhidder joins with the track at a ford by a sheepfold **C**. At the next sheepfold down the glen a rowan tree is growing from the walls of an abandoned shieling. Soon afterwards the reservoir is in view again below, and the track descends steadily, following the stream, to reach the original track **A** which follows the shore. Turn left onto this for the final part of the long walk, which will take about an hour, retracing steps along the track by the reservoir and then past the dam to reach Brig o'Turk.

Red deer stag

Beinn Tharsuinn and Beinn Lochain

Start	Lettermay, Lochgoilhead
Distance	7 miles (11.3km)
Approximate time	5½ hours
Parking	Limited off-road parking at Lettermay
Refreshments	Pubs and restaurants at Lochgoilhead
Ordnance Survey maps	Landranger 56 (Loch Lomond & Inveraray), Pathfinders 367, NN 00/10 (Inveraray & Strachur) and 379, NS 09/19 (Glenbranter)

There is an energetic start to this lovely route around the hills overlooking Lochgoilhead. A stiff climb of about 1400ft (400m) takes walkers above tree level onto the ridge which culminates in Beinn Lochain (2306ft/703m), a craggy summit which is a superlative viewpoint, not only towards Loch Goil but also northwards to Loch Fyne and the mountains beyond. The descent from here demands care, but the walk back passes by a beautiful, remote mountain loch and a spectacular waterfall.

From Lochgoilhead take the road on the western shore of the loch and pass the chalets and caravans of the extensive Leisure Complex. The walk starts from the bridge over the Lettermay Burn and there are parking spaces nearby. Head north up the road from the bridge and turn left to Corrow, a pony-trekking centre. Walk through the yard, go through the gate at the end, and then turn right to begin the demanding climb up to and through a wide firebreak which gives access to the hilltop above the trees. If you have started the walk in the morning and the sun is shining, the view back as you climb is truly dazzling. After about 30 minutes of stiff climbing the worst is over, and the tree-line is below.

Turn left before the rocky outcrops ahead (Creag Loisgte) **A** and follow the contours above the forest, keeping high enough to allow views over the treetops. It would be as well to have a short right leg on this long traverse! Climb to the top of the ridge on the right **B** before coming to the end of the trees for a wonderful panorama. Ben Lomond dominates the view eastwards. Continue heading north-west, towards the col between Stob na Boine Druimfhinn and Beinn Tharsuinn (this is marked as 'Coirein Rathaid', *coirein* being a diminutive form of *coire*). Although mainly pathless, the way up to Beinn Tharsuinn is very obvious, sweeping round to approach the summit from the north-east direction, avoiding a host of hillocks and outcrops. The long summit ridge holds several lochans. It should take about two hours to reach this point **C**.

Having spent time enjoying the grand view and identifying the various summits leave Beinn Tharsuinn on the gentle south-western slope and then swing south to approach Beinn Lochain which at 2287ft (703m) is 249ft (82m) higher than Beinn Tharsuinn. Keep as close to the edge as you dare for the best views (but be careful, for the drop is precipitous and there are many rocky outcrops to skirt). Beinn Lochain has a very modest cairn at its summit **D**, which seems rather insulting for such a wonderful viewpoint. The Curra Lochain nestles below the steepling crags of Beinn Bheula, whose slopes are newly afforested, while to the west Strachur can be seen with Loch Fyne beyond. A succession of grand peaks forms the background of the vista in this direction. To the east and nearer at hand the various summits of the Arrochar Alps are more easily identifiable, particularly the distinctive shape of the Cobbler. All of this breathtaking scenery helps to make the arduous ascent worth while.

The recommended way off Beinn Lochain is to head west until the gradients and outcrops of the ground to the south ease to allow a safe descent. This will mean descending to the top

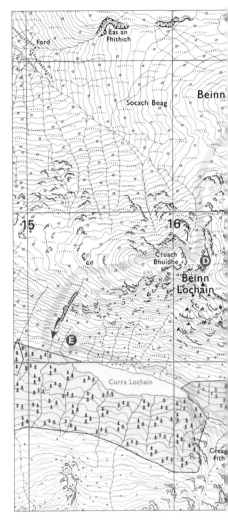

Lettermay Burn with Lochgoilhead in the distance

(western) end of the lochan. The more adventurous may try a more direct descent to its lower end, but there are many cliffs and gullies hidden from above and this may prove risky. Turn left **E** to head eastwards along the rather boggy shore of the remote lochan.

At the lower end of the loch cross over the burn and head down the path on its south-western side. This allows a close-up view of a spectacular waterfall as the Struth Ban drops to join with the

SCALE 1:25000 or 2½ INCHES to 1 MILE 4CM to 1KM

Lettermay Burn **F**. After passing the top of the waterfall the path veers briefly south and then south-east to descend to the new plantings of conifers at the bottom of the valley. Amazingly some of these have been sited so that when they grow they will screen the view of the waterfall from the bottom.

A well-defined path leads through a fence **G** (there is an adjacent stile if the opening is closed) to the banks of another burn which has to be forded. After this an attractive path follows the eastern bank of the Lettermay Burn; Ben Donich is the hill towards which the stream seems to be heading.

At a concrete weir with a pump-house of red brick, turn right **H** onto a forest track which climbs to meet with another in a short distance. Bear left here and continue along it for about a mile as it heads steadily down towards Loch Goil, giving attractive views of the village. Keep a sharp lookout on the left for a firebreak with a path leading to a fence and a track beyond. Take this short cut **J** to reach the track going through a cluster of cottages at Lettermay and follow it to the road. Turn left to return to the start. ●

Ben Vorlich (Loch Earn)

Start	Ardvorlich, on south side of Loch Earn
Distance	7 miles (11.3km)
Approximate time	5½ hours
Parking	Off-road parking on lochside
Refreshments	None
Ordnance Survey maps	Landrangers 51 (Loch Tay) and 57 (Stirling & The Trossachs), Explorer 11 (The Trossachs) and Pathfinder 348, NN 62/72 (Loch Earn & Comrie)

Usually Stuc a' Chroin is 'bagged' at the same time as Ben Vorlich, which is logical if the main aim is climbing Munros. A well-worn path from the summit of Ben Vorlich leads to that of its junior neighbour, and the adventurous could then descend Stuc a' Chroin's south-east ridge to reach the ruined shieling at Dubh Choirein, which is on the footpath leading to Bealach Gliogarsnaich. However, after wet weather there may be difficulty in fording Allt an Dubh Choirein. The route described here leaves Stuc a' Chroin to the more energetic, leading off the summit of Ben Vorlich by the southeastern ridge to descend over rough ground to the path by Allt a' Bhealaich Gliogarsnaiche. At times this is difficult to follow, especially after the bealach which leads into Glen Vorlich. However, there should be no great navigational difficulties in following the burn downstream and the scenery is grand. To check on access during the stalking season telephone 01764 685260.

Hill-walkers use the east driveway at Ardvorlich by the lochside bridge, walking upstream with the Ardvorlich Burn on the right at first. Note that dogs have to be on leads here. Bear right to cross the stream before the farm and then turn left immediately to start climbing up a good track on the west side of the burn.

This is a very pleasant way to climb a hill, following a good clear track up through typical Highland woods. The track forks **A** after a wooden bridge: bear right towards Ben Vorlich.

Cross Allt a' Choire Bhuidhe by another plank bridge **B** and continue to climb directly towards the handsome shape of Ben Vorlich with the stream now below to the right. The path climbs steadily up the flank of the hill's northern ridge. The view opens up well behind with Ben Lawers the commanding summit beyond Loch Earn; at 3982ft (1214m) this is the highest mountain of the Southern

0	200	400	600	800 METRES	1	
						KILOMETRES
						MILES
0	200	400	600 YARDS	½		

Highlands. Nearer the summit the going becomes harder as the path zigzags up very steeply. However, the triangulation pillar soon comes into sight and the reward is a staggering view as befits a mountain of 3231ft (985m). The summit is a level plateau with the triangulation pillar at the north-western end and a large cairn **C** to the south-east, about 100 yards (90m) away.

Walk past the cairn to begin the descent down Vorlich's south-eastern ridge, following a line of old fence posts. When these end, and the path becomes more sketchy, keep following the ridge down until the slope to the left becomes easy enough to allow a descent due east to the Allt a' Bhealaich Gliogarsnaiche **D** (do not leave the ridge too early though, as the outcrops of Cas Dubh are precipitous).

The path from Callander follows this stream northwards into the craggy pass between Ben Vorlich and Beinn Domhnuill – Bealach Gliogarsnaich **E**. Watch for deep and dangerous potholes

The path up to Ben Vorlich

as the faint path climbs up below steepling crags. At best these will fill your boots with water; at worst they will sprain or break an ankle. Note how close the two streams are to 'capturing' each other. The steep and craggy east face of Ben Vorlich is well seen from this point.

From the head of the pass the path is very rudimentary, being more suited for sheep than humans, and following the eastern side of the Ardvorlich Burn which has a series of refreshing cataracts as it flows over rocky ledges. The view ahead is always a delight.

After a lengthy descent the path, such as it is, becomes a track when it meets the remains of a wall **F** below Sgiath a' Phiobaire which is at the tree-line. The track crosses the Allt a' Choire Bhuidhe close to where it joins its waters with those of the Ardvorlich Burn. This is a delightful part of the walk, the way shaded by birch and rowan trees and the stream chuckling close by. The track joins with the one used for the outward journey about a mile (1.6km) above Ardvorlich House. ●

The Brack

Start	Coilessan, near Ardgartan
Distance	9½ miles (15.3km). Alternative version 7½ miles (12.1km)
Approximate time	5 hours (6 hours for the alternative version)
Parking	At end of public road before Coillessan Houses
Refreshments	None
Ordnance Survey maps	Landranger 56 (Loch Lomond & Inveraray) and Pathfinder 368, NN 20/30 (Arrochar & Ben Lomond)

This is an interesting route which apart from twice climbing over the col which separates The Brack from Ben Donich has little in the way of testing gradients, unless you take the option offered here of climbing to the summit of The Brack itself (2582ft, 787m). There are good views of Rest and be Thankful, The Cobbler and Loch Long on both routes, and those liking a long day's walking may wish to continue to Lochgoilhead by way of Glen Donich (see Walk 2).

Turn off the A83 at Ardgartan following the sign to the Youth Hostel and pass timber Forestry Commission buildings. Having crossed the bridge bear right at the junction and continue along the lane for about 2 miles (3.2km) to where the road divides, the left fork going to Coillessan Houses only. Park here and walk up the right-hand road (a made-up forestry track) to reach Cat Craig Road **Ⓐ**.

Turn sharply right along this track to walk parallel to the shore of Loch Long, climbing gradually. Views of the loch open up as the track climbs above the Ardgartan peninsula, where the caravan site and modernistic youth hostel dominate the view across the water to Arrochar. As on so much of this walk, the Cobbler's unmistakable outline commands the view ahead (see Walk 24). From here it is easy to see how the peak acquired its name – try to identify

which of the summits is the Cobbler himself, which is the last over which he bends, and which his wife, who is watching him work.

Cat Craig Road ends at a turning point, its progress halted by a dry ravine **Ⓑ**. Go up steps by a white post to a bridge which crosses the chasm. This bridge is known locally as 'Charlie's Bridge' since it was opened by Prince Charles; it was constructed by unemployed youngsters from Merseyside. Loch Lomond can just be glimpsed from here, beyond Arrochar. The path drops down to another forest track which can be seen twisting along the flank of the glen for miles ahead.

Four miles (6.4km) after the start of this track (or about 80 minutes' walking), with the whole of Rest and be Thankful now in view and after a section of newly cleared forest on the right, keep a sharp watch for a green

0	200	400	600	800 METRES	1	
						KILOMETRES MILES
0	200	400	600 YARDS	½		

forestry waymark on the left **C** which points to the path to Lochgoilhead. This climbs up quite steeply past young trees, though at the top they are more mature. Cross the fence by the stile; from here, dogs must be on leads.

White-topped posts lead the walker up to the Bealach Dubh-lic, the saddle between The Brack (on the left) and Ben Donich (to the right). The cairn is a good place to pause and enjoy the view back: three heights on the far side of Glen Croe are easily identified: Beinn Luibhean, Beinn Ime and Ben Arthur, the last better known as The Cobbler.

The cairn is a false summit and the path continues to climb before the view onward is revealed **D**. The glen ahead looks bleak, and the forest about a mile (1.5km) distant is the next objective unless one has the energy and inclination to climb The Brack – a favourite height with rock-climbers who can tackle routes such as Elephant Gully, the Great Central Groove (conquered only in 1958), the Mammoth, and the Big Game Route. Most of them are classed as 'difficult' or 'severe' climbs.

To follow an alternative route over the Brack, proceed as follows. Descend to the white post at the bottom of the bealach and then climb directly up the

SCALE 1:25 000 or 2½ INCHES to 1 MILE 4CM to 1KM

The view from The Brack

opposing slope, keeping close to the burn. Near the top, traverse to the left to skirt Elephant Gully and the Great Central Groove and reach the summit.

From here go south-south-west, with the summit of Cnoc Coinnich straight ahead at this stage, to find a small burn which threads its way through rocky ground. The going is rough and requires care, especially where the stream drops down through steep gullies (traverse left to avoid the worst of these). Cross a fence and then follow fown the edge of the forest, close to the stream. There is a splendid, refreshing waterfall about halfway down before the path meets a forest track. Cross this and continue down for a short distance to meet with another track, where you turn left on to the longer route.

On the main route, make for the northern (right-hand) edge of the forest to a pointed white-topped post **E** which marks the way over its fence. There is also a stream of sparkling, yet peaty-brown, water to cross – this is the first of many such burns. Initially the path follows a wide firebreak and the way ahead is well seen, wandering past peat banks and hags; great care has to be taken to keep feet dry. The footprints of deer greatly outnumber those left by boots. Beyond a refreshing waterfall the view begins to open up ahead and to the right as The Cobbler is obscured behind.

Soon after you pass a large boulder in the middle of the firebreak a ravine is reached where there is a signpost. Turn left here **F** towards Coilessan and climb up by the stream to reach a stile over the fence, which gives access to open hillside again. Bear slightly to the left having crossed the stile to follow the direction indicated on the waymark. The posts marking the route now have blue tops and it is a strenuous climb following them to the col between The Brack and Cnoc Coinnich. There are very steep cliffs on the south side of The Brack. Pleasant, more level, walking follows to the top cairn **G** which provides a splendid viewpoint. Glen Douglas is well seen on the other side of Loch Long.

From here the path descends steeply to the forest. If you are facing a breeze you will see smoke-like mist to the right where spray is blown back from a waterfall. The path follows the right side of the Coilessan Glen steeply down through the forest, finally crossing the burn and emerging onto a forest track **H**. Bear right here to continue downhill, passing the point where the alternative route rejoins: there are good views as the timber has been harvested. Bear right at the next junction and cross the Coilessan Burn again over a concrete bridge. Carry straight on, keeping to the main track; Arrochar will soon be seen at the head of the loch. Bear left at the next track junction to cross the burn yet again. There are waterfalls here. Beyond this point the road is metalled; bear right when it meets with Cat Craig Road **A** to descend to the starting point.

The Cobbler

Start	Head of Loch Long
Distance	7 miles (11.3km)
Approximate time	6 hours
Parking	Lay-bys on A83 at head of Loch Long
Refreshments	Pubs and tearooms at Arrochar
Ordnance Survey maps	Landranger 56 (Loch Lomond & Inveraray) and Outdoor Leisure 39 (Loch Lomond)

The alpine-like shape of The Cobbler with the fantastic overhang of its north summit can be seen from dozens of viewpoints in the region. As soon as railways provided easy access the Cobbler (it is seldom known by its alternative name of Ben Arthur) was adopted by Glaswegians as a favourite excursion, and the peak has attracted walkers and rock-climbers ever since, even though at 2900ft (884m) it does not quite achieve Munro status.

At the head of Loch Long there are lay-bys on both sides of the A83 which provide convenient (and ever-popular) parking places for this walk. A clear path enters into the trees by the Argyll Forest Park signboard and passes a cairn-like collecting-box for the Arrochar Mountain Rescue team. A steep, eroded path climbs straight up the hillside through the trees, following a line of concrete blocks. When the path emerges onto a forest track, cross straight over this to continue the ascent alongside the blocks, which were the sleepers of a railway which was built to help with the construction of the Loch Sloy Hydro Scheme.

This is a hard slog to gain height quickly; a much more pleasant stretch follows when the steep path meets another running along the flank of the hillside **Ⓐ**. Turn left here. Note the gleaming particles of quartz in the glistening schist, and enjoy the views over Loch Long.

After about 20 minutes' enjoyable walking on this path you arrive at a small dam **Ⓑ** penning back the waters of the Allt a' Bhalachain, and the outline of The Cobbler is suddenly revealed in all its glory. This is a popular spot to rest for a minute or two before continuing to climb – the burn tumbles down over a series of small waterfalls, and the water is cool on feet which are probably already beginning to suffer.

The next part of the route is delightful. The path follows the burn on its course from the mountain. The gradient is easy and the scenery superb, the dramatic outline of the Cobbler becoming more dominant as the mountain is approached.

The two great boulders which are passed on the way up are the Narnain Boulders: rock-climbers find good practice on these, even though the pitches are short. The path crosses the burn **Ⓒ** and bears away from the Coire

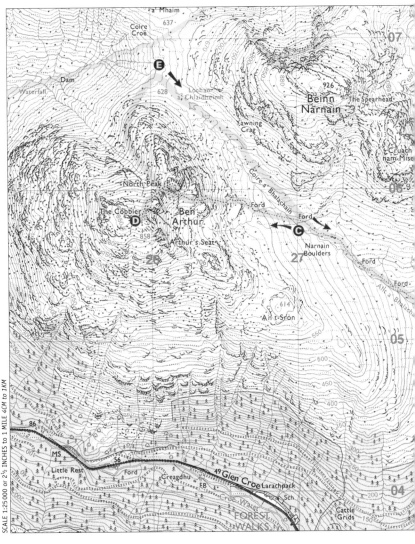

SCALE 1:25 000 or 2½ INCHES to 1 MILE 4CM to 1KM

0	200	400	600	800 METRES	1
					KILOMETRES
					MILES
0	200	400	600 YARDS	½	

a' Bhalachain, soon becoming very steep as the climb up to the summits begins. There is much loose rock (which is even more treacherous in wet conditions) and the popularity of the mountain means the path is becoming very eroded. The final few metres up to the ridge are a good scramble.

From here the view is all-embracing. Ben Lomond is, as ever, an unmistakable landmark. To the north

Beinn Ime blocks the view, though the main road can be seen below its flanks climbing Rest and be Thankful.

Turn to the right along the ridge to climb to the North Peak: of the three peaks this is the only one which – in spite of its incredible nose-like overhangs – is easily accessible to walkers. The infamous central peak (strictly speaking, the name Cobbler refers specifically to this rock) lies in the other direction **D**. Although it is a short and easy climb to reach the base of the rock, getting to the top is another

matter and it is easy to understand why it was made a test of nerve for prospective Campbell chiefs. It entails a scramble up its bare sloping ledges to a rock window, which gives access to another narrow ledge with a drop of hundreds of feet below. This has to be traversed to the left before another brief scramble involving two easy handholds takes you to the flat roof of the summit. As with many such climbs, the way up is easier than the way down.

It is foolish to attempt to come off this mountain by the steep and eroded path used to climb it. Instead, as you return from the central peak walking towards the North Peak look for a distinct path which leaves from near the point where the ridge was reached, and heads north-west. Although this becomes quite steep lower down, it is a straightforward descent leading to the Lochan a' Chlaidheimh, which is almost completely dried out now though its perimeter remains boggy. Turn to the right to reach this **E** and then follow the left bank of the burn, which soon joins with the main path near the

Narnain Boulders. Continue on this down to the dam **B**.

Cross over the stream here and take the path down to the forest, turning to enjoy a last view of the Cobbler before the mountain is obscured by trees – the fantastic overhang is well seen from this point. The path down follows a raised bank with the stream on the left. When the path divides for the first time be sure to bear to the right – the other way is really rugged! There are occasional views of Loch Long below. The stream is never far away and can often be seen dashing over cataracts where there are impressive swirlpools, formed by the erosive force of the stream's waters over countless hundreds of years.

The path down continues though the views are lost once a forestry track is crossed (turn left onto this and follow it to the edge of the forest and the path by the concrete blocks if you prefer to avoid walking by the main road). Towards the bottom there is a fine waterfall where a rock spout makes it possible to actually walk behind the cascading water.

Turn left when the main road is reached and walk back to the starting point at the head of the loch. ●

The Cobbler's central peak

Cruach Ardrain

Start	Glen Falloch, 2 miles (3.2km) south-west of Crianlarich
Distance	7½ miles (12.1km)
Approximate time	6 hours
Parking	Lay-by on south side of A82 opposite Keilator Farm
Refreshments	Tearoom and pubs at Crianlarich
Ordnance Survey maps	Landrangers 50 (Glen Orchy) and 56 (Loch Lomond & Inveraray), Outdoor Leisure 38 (Ben Nevis & Glen Coe) Pathfinder 347, NN 42/52 (Glen Dochart & Lochearnhead)

At 3428ft (1046m) Cruach Ardrain is a formidable Munro whatever the approach. This route tackles it from the north-west and after the demanding initial climb of Grey Height follows a grand ridge walk before the final steep ascent of Cruach Ardrain itself. Instead of the usual long return over Stob Garbh and Stob Coire Bhuidhe (which involves a steep and hazardous descent northwards from Cruach Ardrain) this route takes an easy way down to return along the delightful River Falloch. To check on access during the stalking season telephone 01301 704229.

Take the track which leaves at the north end of the lay-by, twisting down through the meadow to a sheep creep below the railway line and a bridge over the River Falloch. The Land Rover track heads into the glen overlooked by Sròn Gharbh and Meall Dhamh. At the end of the forestry plantings fork left Ⓐ on a track which drops to a bridge across the river. Cross the bridge and begin climbing up the western flank of Grey Height (why a Sassenach name for this hill?) with the forest fence to the left.

The rough grassy slope is taxing but views open up as height is gained. Crianlarich can be seen

beyond the forest and, on the other side of Glen Falloch, the twin peaks of Ben Oss and Beinn Dubhchraig. The top of Grey Height Ⓑ is rocky and the ridge path bypasses the summit as it continues to climb, passing to the east

---

River Falloch and Cruach Ardrain

of Meall Dhamh up to the unnamed summit **C** which overlooks this outlier. There is a lochan just before the top is reached. The massive shape of Cruach Ardrain looks very forbidding ahead as the path threads its way along a ledge with a precipitous drop to Coire Ardrain to the left.

The path drops down steeply to a boggy col where there are stepping-stones across a lochan **D**. Then the steep and direct climb to the summit of Cruach Ardrain begins. As you climb there are views southwards down the narrow Ishag Glen below Stob Glas.

Cruach Ardrain (its name means 'high stack' – perhaps of peat) has a long summit ridge with three cairns, the north-easternmost of these being the summit proper **E**, from which there is a very steep descent to the bealach before Stob Garbh (not attempted on this route, however). The view from each of the cairns is spectacular, with an inviting range of summits seemingly linked to Cruach Ardrain by radiating ridges. This impression is deceptive, though a good path to the south gives a pleasant walk to Beinn Tulaichean – an optional extra if you have enough time and energy.

However, the recommended way is to return westwards (from the western cairn) to the col between Meall Dhamh and Cruach Ardrain. Keep a sharp lookout for a cairn **F** on the right of the path just before the lochan on the bealach. This cairn marks the point at which an easy descent can be made into Coire Earb. You will be heading westwards down grassy slopes towards the darkly spectacular Coire Eich on the other side of the glen, with its silvery threads of cataracts falling to the River Falloch. Small burns springing from the east side of the glen are a welcome source of refreshment after the parched summit ridge.

The craggy outcrops of Meall Dhamh ('hill of the stag') rear above as the bottom of Coire Earb is approached. Sròn Gharbh looks a challenging top on the other side of the glen. On the eastern side there is a lone tree: pass close to this on the descent. The Land

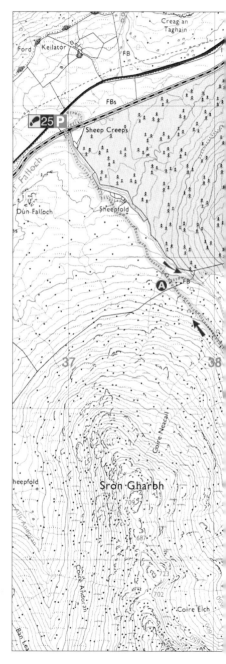

Rover track can be seen in the far distance. There are many summer flowers on the lower hillside and by the banks of the burn (the infant River Falloch). A crossing point **G** should be found before the stream grows, and the faint and often boggy path on the western side eventually leads to a sheepfold **H** which is the terminus of the Land Rover track returning down the glen to the main road.

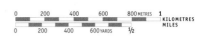

SCALE 1:25000 or 2½ INCHES to 1 MILE 4CM to 1KM

Ben Lomond from Rowardennan

Start	Rowardennan
Distance	7½ miles (12.1km)
Approximate time	5 hours
Parking	Car park at Rowardennan Pier
Refreshments	Hotel at Rowardennan
Ordnance Survey maps	Landranger 56 (Loch Lomond & Inveraray) and Outdoor Leisure 39 (Loch Lomond

If you spend any time in the area you will find yourself – like generations before you – almost inevitably drawn towards Ben Lomond and its ascent. Its name is thought to derive from an old word (Ilumnan) meaning 'beacon' and is very apposite as it is seen from all around, which also means that on a clear day the views from its summit are extensive in all directions.

The main route to the summit is that from Rowardennan; on a fine day in summer it is little more than a strenuous uphill walk on a well-established path (and mountain-runners make the ascent and descent in just over an hour!). In winter, however, it can become a serious expedition when snow and ice make an ice-axe and crampons necessary equipment, and at all times of the year strong winds and a marked temperature drop may be experienced as the summit is approached. Rowardennan itself is at the end of an unclassified road which often becomes congested with traffic, but the long (albeit attractive) drive from the west side of Loch Lomond can be avoided in summer by using the ferry crossing from Inverbeg.

From the car park take the path directly behind the public toilets which is signed 'Ben Lomond Path'; in about 150 yds (140m) join a path coming up from the right and continue up a wide ride (ie. a gap between the forestry planting) between larch trees on the right and predominantly sitka spruce on the left. The gradient varies as one ascends through the forest, but the path is well constructed with a bridge over a small burn and rock steps in a steep section. There are occasional views to the left across Loch Lomond to the hills beyond, and also up to the summit of Ben Lomond and the secondary peak of Ptarmigan to its left. After ¾ mile (1.2km) a gate **Ⓐ** is reached at the top of the forest.

You are now passing onto land owned by the National Trust for Scotland; this is used for sheep grazing, and dogs must be kept on a lead. Grazing has a considerable effect on the vegetation – note the contrasting regenerated woodland in Coire Corrach to the left where sheep have been excluded by fencing. The Ben Lomond footpath is used by many thousands of walkers every year and work is undertaken to repair and improve it: foundations have been provided made of matting or rock, and some of the gradients eased by zigzagging, but most significantly drainage has been provided to reduce the erosion by water of loose material which is continually exposed by the pounding of many pairs of walking-boots.

If you pause to look back, perhaps at the gate in the next fence **B**, you will see Inverbeg on the other side of the loch, with the sizeable delta at the mouth of Douglas Water and the wild Luss hills rising beyond. The many islands (Inches) of Loch Lomond are seen in its wider southern part. The Highland Boundary Fault runs through

The view from the summit of Ben Lomond

the largest of these, Inchmurrin, and then Creinch, Torrinch and Inchcailloch; this is the fault line that separates the northern older rocks of the Highlands – remnants of the great Caledonian Mountain Chain – from the much younger rocks of the Central Valley of Scotland (see Walk 7).

As you continue upwards onto Sròn Aonaich  views of the Trossachs open up to the right with Loch Ard and Ben Venue identifiable. From here the gradient eases for a while and the path is marked by cairns which, while common in mountain areas of England and Wales, are comparatively rare in Scotland, where the hill-walker is expected to be able to find the way without such aids! Across Loch Lomond to the west-north-west the craggy profile of the Cobbler, amongst the Arrochar Alps, becomes increasingly visible as you ascend.

It remains to tackle the steep final section of the ascent to reach the point on the path ⬤ where it attains the ridge running east-south-east from the summit, and where the views of the mountains to the north across Loch Katrine suddenly appear – a visual reward for the uphill toil! The path continues well below the crest of the ridge and rises fairly easily now to gain the summit of the Ben ⬤ at 3194ft (974m). From here the Highland mountains seem to rise endlessly to the north and west, contrasting with the views south to the Central Valley and even to the hills of the Borders, the Clyde estuary with a glimpse of some enticing islands beyond to the south-west, and lower hills such as the Campsies to the south-east.

The descent is mainly by the same route, but those with sure feet and a head for heights can follow the crest of the ridge to point ⬤, looking over the crags down into Coire a' Bhathaich. As you continue downwards on the main path the views in front and to each side can now be appreciated without the need to stop and turn round.

A further alternative route, for the final part of the descent through the forest, is available for those who would appreciate some variety. Pass through the gate at point ⬤ and carefully estimate 260 yds (240m) along the path from here, perhaps counting your paces. This should bring you to a point where, beneath the conifers, a path descends through the trees on the right; it is not at all obvious at the start and you may have to peer underneath the trees to see it, but you may also find a notch on a tree at the point where you turn down, which will confirm identification of the path. It quickly becomes more evident as you proceed, swinging first right and then left to emerge above a valley with the sound of a waterfall getting ever nearer. The path continues along a terrace, with the valley on the right, and views of the waterfall open up behind. Proceed through the woods with a last glimpse of the river, Ardess Burn, as it tumbles through a small gorge, and a little further on you will see a brick tank to your right. Keep to the left here; follow the path which goes on to pass between an earth bank (left) and a ruined fence (right). About 380 yds (350m) after the tank the path passes beneath an overhead power line and bears left to ascend a short way before crossing over a small burn. The final section leads downhill through some beautiful ancient oakwoods (declared a Forest Nature Reserve in 1989) with an incised valley to the left of the path, and reaches a gravel road ⬤ about $^1/_4$ mile (400m) north of the car park from which you started.

The Ben Cruachan Horseshoe

Start	Cruachan power station
Distance	8 miles (12.9km)
Approximate time	8 hours
Parking	Lay-bys on main road near power station
Refreshments	None
Ordnance Survey maps	Landranger 50 (Glen Orchy), Pathfinders 345, NN 02/12 (Loch Awe North) and 332, NN 03/13 (Glen Kinglass)

Make no mistake: this route provides a major challenge even for the experienced walker. The total height climbed in walking the seven summits is well over 5000ft (1524m) and the rocky parts of the traverse require some scrambling. Perhaps the worst of it is that the climbing is not finished even when Ben Cruachan has been captured: the route down takes in the lesser summit of Meall Cuanail, a formidable obstacle after what has come before. Man has adapted the landscape here to his own needs and the great reservoir is testament to this. The most remarkable part of this work, however, is screened from view below the waters of Loch Awe and beneath the mountain itself – this is sometimes called the Hollow Mountain because of the chamber excavated inside it to house the generators. At some point try to make time to visit the Cruachan power station: it will be all the more impressive if you have intimate knowledge of the mountain which gives it both its name and the water to power its turbines. To check on access to this route during the stalking season telephone 01838 200217.

The obvious place to park would seem to be the Visitors' Centre car park at the power station, but since it closes at 4.45pm it is of little use to climbers undertaking this demanding route. There is off-road parking reasonably close to the start.

The route begins at a track which leaves the main road opposite the staff car park of the power station, about 100 yards (90m) east of the entrance to the public car park. The track gives access to a railway crossing through a kissing-gate. Then a path climbs steeply up the west bank of a burn, oaks and birches screening the view at first. However, after a few minutes it will be necessary to pause for breath, and by this time

The reservoir from Ben Cruachan

enough height will have been gained to allow views over Loch Awe. This is a steep and unrelenting ascent accompanied by the soothing sound of the burn, which is never very far distant.

The best views back are from the tree-line where the path levels out. If the burn is not in spate it is possible to cut a corner here **A** by heading for the pylon below the hydro road on the right, climbing up a grassy bank from the stream to reach the road and thus avoiding a dog-leg. Turn left onto the road and then fork right to reach the eastern side of Cruachan Reservoir. Before the tunnel entrance **B** (where the track ends) climb a little way up the slopes of the hill and then follow the contours northwards.

Keep fairly low on the flank of the hill to ford two streams, the second, major, one coming down from Lairig Torran, the access point for the ridge. Make the most of the cold sparkling water here **C**: there are few streams once the ridge is gained.

The climbing is steady from here, eastwards, following the stream at first up a grassy slope. Beyond the source of the burn is the Lairig Torran, a pass used by drovers before the building of

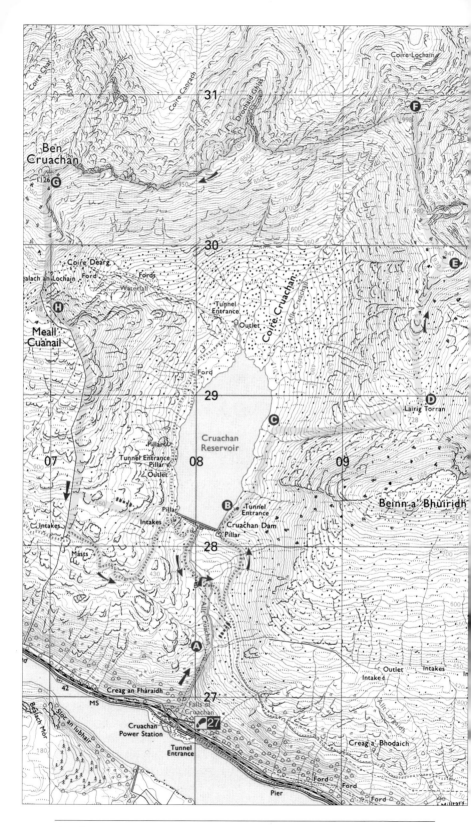

the reservoir. In those days the ground now covered by water was valuable summer pasture. Turn northwards at the col  and continue to climb, making for a cairn on the skyline which sports a metal post from its centre. This is one of several false summits, but soon afterwards you will be on the ridge enjoying a fabulous view which extends over most of the Southern Highlands. Beinn Bhuidhe is the dominant summit to the south-east.

Although the ridge looks daunting, walking along it is exhilarating. For about 200 yds (182m) the path which heads northwards is level, but then it loses itself amongst scattered rock before the climb to the first notable summit. After this there are precipitous slopes to the right; snow can remain piled against these crags until midsummer. Each succeeding summit offers a better view. After a cairn the path drops down steeply amongst boulders – in places it is becoming eroded. There is a handsome cairn on top of the next ridge – above Coire Lochain – where the path swings through 90° to head west. Loch Etive can be seen now, and, on a clear day, Ben Nevis. This height can suffer badly from midges, even in May with snow still on the ground.

From here the route descends to an exciting feature – a narrow ridge hardly wider than Striding Edge in the Lake District. After the last level section of this skywalk the path disintegrates and the walker is left with a scramble to surmount the massive scattered boulders of Drochaid Ghlas. It is important to keep to the path (such as it is) even though it comes close to the edge at times. Now the summit of Cruachan is revealed in all its glory.

After a short easy stretch along a ridge only a few metres wide the final assault on the summit commences. Smooth boulders left tilted at steep angles present a challenging obstacle, and some may feel the best way to tackle them is in an undignified seated position. The top of Ben Cruachan is only a short scramble away from this last hazard to ankles and nerves.

The view is outstanding: on a clear day the distinctive domed shape of Ben Nevis is easily identifiable to the north, as is the conical form of Ben Starav to the north-east, though some closer heights are less easy to recognise. All of Loch Etive and most of Loch Awe can also be seen.

However, there is one summit which is almost too easy to identify and which has been lurking menacingly at the back of the mind ever since the ridge was reached. To get off Ben Cruachan one last peak has to be claimed – Meall Cuanail – and after this time and distance its steep slope looks formidable. It may be for this reason that people do not linger long on the summit of Cruachan. The way down is difficult at first, steep and over loose rock. It improves towards the bottom, where there is an opportunity to refresh hot feet in the cool waters of a lochan.

From the top of Meall Cuanail follow the fence which has led up from the lochan down to the track by the radio masts, and follow this to the dam (it is possible to cut a corner here by heading towards the western end of the dam before reaching the track, though the way down is quite difficult over tussocky grass). Follow the track away from the dam, without crossing the stream (the Allt Cruachan), but turn off to the right just before the bridge, by a wooden post, to retrace steps down the path to the railway and then the starting point.

Ben More and Stob Binnein

Start	Glen Dochart
Distance	10 miles (16.1km)
Approximate time	8 hours
Parking	In lay-by on A85 just to west of bridge over Allt Coire Chaorach, about 5 miles (8km) east of Crianlarich
Refreshments	None
Ordnance Survey maps	Landranger 51 (Loch Tay) and Pathfinder 347, NN 42/52 (Glen Dochart & Lochearnhead)

This route demands both stamina and some skill in navigation. It is not so much a walk as a challenge, entailing an ascent of 4900ft (1500m) in total, and covering a distance of 10 miles (16km), much of it over steep, rough, trackless ground. Bear in mind that if you are on the hill at 9am it may well be two in the afternoon before you reach the first of the summits. The views from the tops are stunning (said to encompass half of Scotland) and for this reason alone it is worth saving a good day for the expedition. To attempt it in poor visibility would be asking for disaster. To check on access during the stalking season telephone 01567 820487.

From the lay-by walk across the bridge to a gate on the right. This gives access to a track leading through a meadow (once the site of Rob Roy's house) to a green gate into the forest. The track through the forest is very gloomy but lightens when it comes to a ford **A**, where it is difficult to keep dry feet even in times of drought. Stepping-stones and overhanging branches are helpful. In fact there is a hazard of wet feet throughout this approach, with the path suffering from the passage of many pairs of boots.

After crossing the ford turn left along the west bank of Allt Coire Chaorach. Another sparkling burn is crossed in a refreshing glade – at this point the path is some way from the major stream, though it soon swings back to the south-east towards it. However, the path emerges from the forest **B** with the stream some distance to the east. It takes about an hour to reach this point. The elegant Stob Binnein and less gainly, more massive, Ben More are revealed standing majestically above the vast corrie; the route runs round the rim of this enormous basin.

Bear left across the valley over broken ground, and cross the stream and deer fence near sheep pens before attacking the climb up to the north-eastern arm of the ridge. This is the start of an unrelenting struggle up virtually pathless slopes. The first minor summit,

Leacann Riabhach, is a teaser with a succession of false summits while Stob Creagach ⒸⒼ, which follows, also has its share of these. However, it is not necessary to follow the crest of the ridge, and energy will be saved by choosing a route which does not have too many descents.

Ben More from Strath Fillan

From Stob Creagach the mountain wilderness to the east is revealed. The route drops slightly to the Bealach na Frithe before the stiff climb up to Meall na Dige – the first 3000-footer though not a Munro in its own right. Keen-eyed walkers will find traces of a path along the ridge which drops abruptly down to a lochan 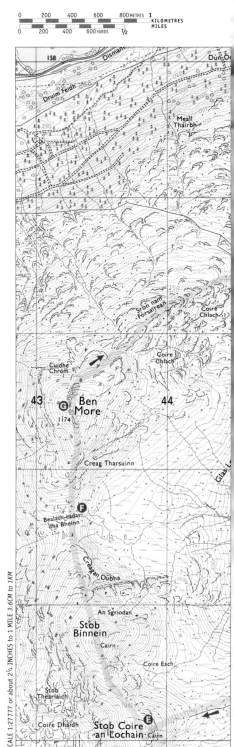, the prelude to a demanding climb to Stob Coire an Lochain, the first stage of the ascent of Stob Binnein ('anvil peak').

Keep the remains of a wall to the left as you climb the ridge, taking time to draw breath and admire the views, which are magnificent here but even better from the top cairn. A lovely lochan just below the summit gives this height its name, and the Stob Binnein path (now very distinct) passes the left side of this peak, dropping to a narrow col before climbing steeply to the next summit.

The only thing that mars the conquering of Stob Binnein is the prospect of the ascent of Ben More, which looks steep and forbidding from here, though this is actually deceptive. The last part of the climb up the Stob is very exciting, the best part of the route. Ben More appears much more shapely from Stob Binnein and serves as an impressive foreground for views to the north. From here the path is quite distinct, though steep and rocky, and the 1000-foot (300m) final climb up to the major summit from Bealach-eadar-dha Bheinn should take only 30 minutes or so if all is going well. Crianlarich comes into view as height is gained, and from the summit it is easy to believe the claim that in ideal conditions the panorama takes in half of Scotland, from Edinburgh to the islands off the west coast (as well as the north coast of Ireland – Ben More is easily identified from the Giant's Causeway), and from Galloway to the

SCALE 1:27777 or about 2¼ INCHES to 1 MILE 3.6CM to 1KM

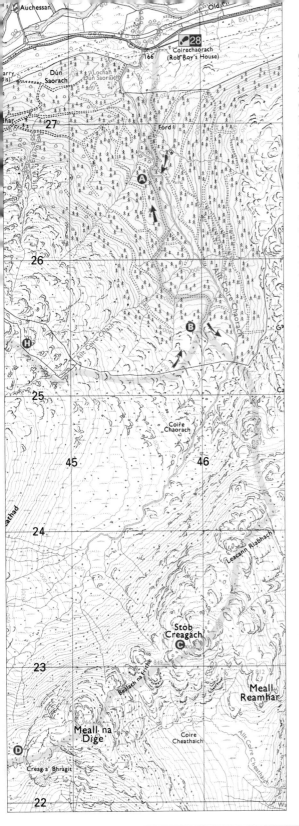

Cairngorm peaks. Ben More is the highest summit in Britain south of Strathtay and the biggest mountain in the Southern Highlands after Ben Lawers. Its name means, quite simply, 'big mountain'.

Leave by the north-east ridge heading as though to Loch Tay. Keep to the left of a boulder-field (there is a cairn just before this) and at the rocky outcrop on the far side of it veer slightly left to find a narrow rocky path which runs along the northern edge of the ridge. This avoids several steep scrambles which would be encountered on the crest.

Continue to follow the ridge until you can see an easy way down to the deer fence (inevitably this means crossing rough ground). Turn right at the fence **H** and follow it back towards the forest. At this stage of the outing this section may seem interminable, crossing acres of hummocky bog, but eventually you will reach an opening in the fence with a clear Land Rover track heading towards the gap in the forest from which you emerged **B**, fresh as a daisy, some hours earlier. Once in the forest again follow the clear (albeit often waterlogged) path back to the start. ●

Further Information

The Law and Tradition as they affect Walking in Scotland

Walkers following the routes given in this book should not run into problems, but it is as well to know something about the law as it affects access, and also something of the traditions which can be quite different in Scotland from elsewhere in Britain. Most of this is common sense, observing the country code and having consideration for others and their activities, which may be their livelihood.

It is often said that there is no law of trespass in Scotland. In fact there is, but the trespass itself is not usually a criminal offence. You can be asked to leave any property, and technically 'reasonable force' may be used to obtain your compliance – though the term is not defined! You can be charged with causing damage due to the trespass, but this would be hard to establish if you were just walking on open, wild, hilly country where, whatever the law, in practice there has been a long tradition of free access for recreational walking – something both the Scottish Landowners' Federation and the Mountaineering Council of Scotland do not want to see changed.

There are certain restrictions. Walkers should obey the country code and seasonal restrictions arising from lambing or stalking. Where there is any likelihood of such restrictions this is mentioned in the text and visitors are asked to comply. When camping, use a campsite. Camp fires should not be lit; they are a danger to moorland and forest, and really not necessary as lightweight and efficient stoves are now available.

Many of the walks in this book are on rights of way. The watchdog on rights of way in Scotland is the Scottish Rights of Way Society (SRWS), who maintain details on all established cases and will, if need be, contest attempted closures. They produce a booklet on the Scottish legal position (Rights of Way, A Guide to the Law in Scotland, 1991), and their green signposts are a familiar sight by many footpaths and tracks, indicating the lines of historic routes.

The River Lochay from the old railway bridge

In Scotland rights of way are not marked on Ordnance Survey maps as is the case south of the border. It was not felt necessary to show these as such on the maps – a further reflection of the freedom to roam that is enjoyed in Scotland. So a path on a map is no indication of a right of way, and many paths and tracks of great use to walkers were built by estates as stalking paths or for private access. While you may traverse such paths, taking due care to avoid damage to property and the natural environment, you should obey restricted access notices and leave if asked to do so.

The only established rights of way are those where a court case has resulted in a legal judgment, but there are thousands of other 'claimed' rights of way. Local planning authorities have a duty to protect rights of way – no easy task with limited resources. Many attempts at closing claimed rights of way have been successfully contested in the courts by the Scottish Rights of Way Society and local authorities.

A dog on a lead or under control may also be taken on a right of way. There is little chance of meeting a free-range solitary bull on any of the walks. Any herds seen are not likely to be dairy cattle, but all cows can be inquisitive and may approach walkers, especially if they have a dog. Dogs running among stock may be shot on the spot; this is not draconian legislation but a desperate attempt to stop sheep and lambs being harmed, driven to panic or lost, sometimes with fatal results. Any practical points or restrictions will be given in the text of each walk. If there is no comment it can be assumed that the route carries no real restrictions.

Scotland in fact likes to keep everything as natural as possible, so, for instance, waymarking is kept to a minimum (the Scottish Rights of Way Society signposts and Forest Walk markers are in unobtrusive colours). In Scotland people are asked to 'walk softly in the wilderness, to take nothing except photographs, and leave nothing except footprints' – which is better than any law.

Scotland's Hills and Mountains: a Concordat on Access

This remarkable agreement was published early in 1996 and is likely to have considerable influence on walkers' rights in Scotland in the future. The signatories include organisations which have formerly been at odds - the Scottish Landowners' Federation and the Ramblers' Association, for example. However they joined with others to make the Access Forum (a full list of signatories is detailed below). The RSPB and the National Trust for Scotland did not sign the Concordat initially but it is hoped that they will support its principles.

The signatories of the Concordat are:

Association of Deer Management Groups
Convention of Scottish Local Authorities
Mountaineering Council of Scotland
National Farmers' Union of Scotland
Ramblers' Association Scotland
Scottish Countryside Activities Council
Scottish Landowners' Federation
Scottish Natural Heritage
Scottish Sports Association
Scottish Sports Council

They agreed that the basis of access to the hills for the purposes of informal recreation should be:

Freedom of access exercised with responsibility and subject to reasonable constraints for management and conservation purposes.

Acceptance by visitors of the needs of land management, and understanding of how this sustains the livelihood, culture and community interests of those who live and work in the hills.

Acceptance by land managers of the public's expectation of having access to the hills.

Acknowledgment of a common interest in the natural beauty and special qualities of Scotland's hills, and the need to work together for their protection and enhancement.

Further Information

The Forum point out that the success of the Concordat will depend on all who manage or visit the hills acting on these four principles. In addition, the parties to the Concordat will promote good practice in the form of:

Courtesy and consideration at a personal level.

A welcome to visitors.

Making advice readily available on the ground or in advance.

Better information about the uplands and hill land uses through environmental education.

Respect by visitors for the welfare needs of livestock and wildlife.

Glossary of Gaelic Names

Most of the place-names in this region are Gaelic in origin, and this list gives some of the more common elements, which will allow readers to understand otherwise meaningless words and appreciate the relationship between place-names and landscape features. Place-names often have variant spellings, and the more common of these are given here.

aber	mouth of loch, river	eilidh	hind
abhainn	river	eòin, eun	bird
allt	stream	fionn	white
auch, ach	field	fraoch	heather
bal, bail, baile	town, homestead	gabhar, ghabhar,	
bàn	white, fair, pale	gobhar	goat
bealach	hill pass	garbh	rough
beg, beag	small	geal	white
ben, beinn	hill	ghlas, glas	grey
bhuidhe	yellow	gleann, glen	narrow, valley
blar	plain	gorm	blue, green
brae, braigh	upper slope, steepening	inbhir, inver	confluence
		inch, inis, innis	island, meadow by river
breac	speckled		
cairn	pile of stones, often marking a summit	lag, laggan	hollow
		làrach	old site
cam	crooked	làirig	pass
càrn	cairn, cairn-shaped hill	leac	slab
		liath	grey
caol, kyle	strait	loch	lake
ceann, ken, kin	head	lochan	small loch
cil, kil	church, cell	màm	pass, rise
clach	stone	maol	bald-shaped top
clachan	small village	monadh	upland, moor
cnoc	hill, knoll, knock	mór, mor(e)	big
coille, killie	wood	odhar, odhair	dun-coloured
corrie, coire, choire	mountain hollow	rhu, rubha	point
		ruadh	red, brown
craig, creag	cliff, crag	sgòr, sgòrr, sgùrr	pointed
crannog, crannag	man-made island	sron	nose
dàl, dail	field, flat	stob	pointed
damh	stag	strath	valley (broader than glen)
dearg	red		
druim, drum	long ridge	tarsuinn	traverse, across
dubh, dhu	black, dark	tom	hillock (rounded)
dùn	hill fort	tòrr	hillock (more rugged)
eas	waterfall	tulloch, tulach	knoll
eilean	island	uisge	water, river

Loch Long and the Arrochar Alps from Doune Hill

Adherence to relevant codes and standards of good practice by visitors and land managers alike.

Any local restrictions on access should be essential for the needs of management, should be fully explained, and be for the minimum period and area required.

Queries should be addressed to:
Access Forum Secretariat, c/o Recreation and Access Branch, Scottish Natural Heritage, 2 Anderson Place, Edinburgh EH6 5NP.

Safety on the Hills

The Highland hills and lower but remote areas call for care and respect. The idyllic landscape of the tourist brochures can change rapidly into a world of gales, rain and mist, potentially lethal for those ill-equipped or lacking navigational skills. The Scottish hills in winter can be arctic in severity, and even in summer, snow can lash the summits. It is essential that the walker is aware of these hazards, which are discussed more fully in the introduction.

At the very least carry adequate wind- and waterproof outer garments, food and drink to spare, a basic first-aid kit, whistle, map and compass – and know how to use them. Wear boots. Plan within your capabilities. If going alone ensure you leave details of your proposed route. Heed local advice, listen to weather forecasts, and do not hesitate to modify plans if conditions deteriorate.

Some of the walks in this book venture into remote country and others climb high summits, and these expeditions should only be undertaken in good summer conditions. In winter they could well need the skills and experience of mountaineering rather than walking. In midwinter the hours of daylight are of course much curtailed, but given crisp, clear late-winter days many of the shorter expeditions would be perfectly feasible, if the guidelines given are adhered to. THINK is the only actual rule. Your life may depend on that. Seek to learn more about the Highlands and your part in them, and continue to develop your skills and broaden your experience.

Mountain Rescue
In case of emergency the standard procedure is to dial 999 and ask for the police who will assess and deal with the situation.

First, however, render first aid as required and make sure the casualty is made warm and comfortable. The distress signal (six flashes/whistle-blasts, repeated at minute intervals) may bring help from other walkers in the area. Write down essential details: exact location (six-figure reference), time of accident, numbers involved, details of injuries, steps already taken; then despatch a messenger to phone the police.

If leaving the casualty alone, mark the site with an eye-catching object. Be patient; waiting for help can seem interminable.

Further Information

Useful Organisations

Association for the Protection of Rural Scotland
Gladstone's Land, 3rd floor,
483 Lawnmarket,
Edinburgh EH1 2NT
Tel. 0131 225 7012

Forestry Commission
Information Department,
231 Corstorphine Road,
Edinburgh EH12 7AT
Tel. 0131 334 0303
Aberfoyle District: 01877 382383
Cowal Forest District: 01369 840666
Loch Awe Forest District: 01546 602518

Historic Scotland
Longmore House,
Salisbury Place,
Edinburgh EH9 1SH
Tel. 0131 668 8600

Loch Lomond Park Authority Ranger Service
Tel. 01389 758216

Stob Binnein from Stob Coire an Lochain

Long Distance Walkers' Association
10 Temple Park Close, Leeds,
West Yorkshire LS15 0JJ
Tel. 0113 264 2205

Mountaineering Council of Scotland
71 King Street (Flat 1R), Crieff PH7 3HB
Tel. 01764 654962

Mountain Rescue Posts in the Southern Highlands
Arrochar Outdoor Centre: 01301 702355
Police Station, Crianlarich: 01838 300222
Dounans Camp School,
Aberfoyle: 01877 382291

National Trust for Scotland
5 Charlotte Square, Edinburgh EH2 4DU
Tel. 0131 226 5922

Ordnance Survey
Romsey Road, Southampton SO16 4GU
Tel. 0345 330011 (Lo-call)

Ramblers' Association (main office)
1/5 Wandsworth Road, London SW8 2XX
Tel. 0171 582 6878

Ramblers' Association (Scotland)
23 Crusader House, Haig Business Park,
Markinch, Fife KY7 6AQ
Tel. 01592 611177

Royal Society for the
Protection of Birds
Abernethy Forest Reserve, Forest Lodge,
Nethybridge, Inverness-shire PH25 3EF
Tel. 01479 821409

Scottish Landowners' Federation
25 Maritime Street, Edinburgh EH6 5PW
Tel. 0131 555 1031

Scottish Natural Heritage
12 Hope Terrace, Edinburgh EH9 2AS
Tel. 0131 556 8400

Scottish Rights of Way Society Ltd
Unit 2, John Cotton Business Centre,
10 Sunnyside, Edinburgh EH7 5RA
Tel. 0131 652 2937

Scottish Wildlife Trust
Cramond House, Kirk Cramond,
Cramond Glebe Road, Edinburgh EH4 6NS
Tel. 0131 312 7765

Scottish Youth Hostels Association
7 Glebe Crescent, Stirling FK8 2JA
Tel. 01786 451181

Weather Forecasts
Mountaincall (Highlands West):
0891 500441
Mountaincall (Highlands East):
0891 500442
Scotland seven-day forecast: 0891 112260
UK seven-day forecast Tel. 0891 333123

Tourist Information
Scottish Tourist Board
23 Ravelston Terrace, Edinburgh EH4 3EU
Tel. 0131 332 2433
Loch Lomond, Stirling &
Trossachs Tourist Board
41 Dumbarton Road, Stirling FK8 2QQ
Tel. 01786 475019
Local tourist information offices:
Callander: 01877 330342
Dumbarton: 01389 743206
Dunoon: 01369 703785
Glasgow: 0141 204 4400
Gourock: 01475 639467
Helensburgh: 01436 672642
Oban: 01631 563122

Ordnance Survey Maps of Loch Lomond and the Trossachs

This area is covered by Ordnance Survey
1:50 000 ($1\frac{1}{4}$ inches to 1 mile or 2cm to
1km) scale Landranger map sheets 49, 50,
51, 55, 56, 57 and 64. These all-purpose
maps are packed with information to help
you explore the area. Viewpoints, picnic
sites, places of interest and caravan and
camping sites are shown, as well as public
rights-of-way information such as
footpaths and bridleways.

To examine the Loch Lomond and
Trossachs area in more detail, and
especially if you are planning walks,
Ordnance Survey Outdoor Leisure maps 38
(Ben Nevis & Glen Coe) and 39 (Loch
Lomond) at 1:25 000 ($2\frac{1}{2}$ inches to 1 mile
or 4cm to 1km) are ideal. Explorer map 11
(The Trossachs) at 1:25 000 scale also
covers the area.

The following Pathfinder maps
complete the coverage of the area at
1:25 000 scale:

331 (NM 83/93)	359 (NN 61/71)
332 (NN 03/13)	367 (NN 00/10)
334 (NN 43/53)	368 (NN 20/30)
343 (NM 62/72)	370 (NN 60/70)
344 (NM 82/92)	378 (NR 99)
345 (NN 02/12)	379 (NS 09/19)
347 (NN 42/52)	380 (NS 29/39)
348 (NN 62/72)	381 (NS 49/59)
355 (NM 81/91)	389 (NS 08/18)
356 (NN 01/11)	390 (NS 28/38)
357 (NN 21/31)	391 (NS 48/58)

To get to Loch Lomond and the
Trossachs use the Ordnance Survey Great
Britain Routeplanner Travelmaster map
number 1 at 1:625 000 (1 inch to 10 miles
or 1cm to 6.25km) scale or Travelmaster
map 4 (Central Scotland and
Northumberland) at 1:250 000 (1 inch to 4
miles or 1cm to 2.5km) scale.

Ordnance Survey maps and guides are
available from most booksellers, stationers
and newsagents.

Index

Entries in italics refer to illustrations